WHAT MAKES A CARMELITE A CARMELITE?

Studies in the Carmelite Tradition

WHAT MAKES

A CARMELITE

A CARMELITE?

Exploring Carmel's Charism

KEITH J. EGAN

Introduction by Steven Payne, OCD

*The 2020 Annual Lecture in Carmelite Studies at
The Catholic University of America*

The Catholic University of America Press
Washington, D.C.

Library of Congress Control Number: 2022946859

ISBN: 978-0-8132-3628-5

eISBN: 978-0-8132-3629-2

WHAT MAKES A CARMELITE A CARMELITE?

Contents

INTRODUCTION TO

"WHAT MAKES

A CARMELITE A CARMELITE?"

As the current Chair of Carmelite Studies at The Catholic University of America, I am very pleased to introduce not only our inaugural "Annual Lecture in Carmelite Studies" but also the first in what we hope will be a major new series of "Studies in the Carmelite Tradition." This important talk by the dean of contemporary North American Carmelite scholarship, Professor Keith J. Egan, explores the fundamental question of Carmelite identity, how the charism evolved under the guidance of the Spirit, and what this might reveal more broadly about similar processes involving other community charisms in the church.[1] May it mark

---

1   The lecture was originally scheduled for October 2020, but the actual delivery had to be postponed until February 2021, due to the COVID pandemic.

the beginning of a long and fruitful collaboration between the Center and Catholic University of America Press!

About the Center

This introduction to our 2020 lecture also offers a providential opportunity to introduce the background and mission of the Catholic University of America's new Center for Carmelite Studies. It was officially launched on October 15, 2019, but its inspiration can be traced back to earlier developments at the former Washington Theological Union (WTU), located a few miles from Catholic University. For many years, under the guidance of Very Rev. John Welch, O.Carm., and the Carmelites, WTU offered a graduate certificate in Carmelite Studies that attracted students from around the world and was also available in a distance-learning mode. There were hopes that other Carmelite programs could be added in the future. When the Union finally closed operations in 2015, however, the Carmelite Studies certificate was orphaned. Some of its courses migrated for a time to Catholic University, but they were not easily sustainable without a particular academic program or center anchoring them. Accordingly, the Carmelite Province of the Most Pure Heart of Mary was looking for the best way forward to ensure the future of Carmelite Studies in the United States. After much discussion and reflection, they agreed to sponsor an endowed Chair and Center of Carmelite Studies at Catholic University, with the mission of "making the resources of the rich Carmelite heritage available to the contemporary church and world, by fostering scholarly study and research in the history, culture, and spirituality of the Carmelites, and promoting the effective pastoral application of the results"[2]

---

2   This text is adapted from the description of the mission of the Center for Carmelite Studies on its website.

About the Carmelite Tradition

But what exactly is this "Carmelite tradition" and what is its scope? Not so long ago, the contribution of Carmel was mainly identified with its mystical spirituality, and its mystical spirituality was identified with Saints Teresa of Ávila and John of the Cross. One reason for this is that, ironically, Carmelites were the victims of their own success. With the rise of baroque scholasticism, a series of Discalced Carmelite scholars in the seventeenth and eighteenth centuries expended enormous energy carefully systematizing the teachings of these two Spanish mystics into influential multi-volume works in the scholastic mold. As Bernard McGinn has noted: "If one looks back at the history of [the] modern Catholic study of mysticism . . . , it is clear that Teresa and John exercised a preponderant role in what Neoscholastic thought identified as mysticism, one similar to Thomas's position in dogmatic and speculative theology."[3] Unfortunately, this meant that into the first half of the twentieth-century seminarians and theology students were exposed to the Carmelite heritage almost exclusively through "proof texts" in manuals of mystical theology drawn from the writings of Teresa and John, who were cited rarely if ever in other areas of the theological curriculum. Such an approach, despite genuine intellectual achievements, eventually exhausted itself in increasingly abstruse analyses, now largely forgotten.[4]

---

3   Bernard McGinn, "The Role of the Carmelites in the History of Western Mysticism," in *Carmel and Contemplation: Transforming Human Consciousness,* ed. Kevin Culligan and Regis Jordan, Carmelite Studies 8 (Washington, D.C.: ICS Publications, 2000), 45. See also Bernard McGinn, *Mysticism in the Golden Age of Spain (1500–1650),* vol. 1, part 2 of *The Presence of God: A History of Western Mysticism* (New York: Herder & Herder 2017), viii–ix, 208.

4   This baroque scholastic approach reached its zenith in the eighteenth century in Joseph of the Holy Spirit, *Cursus Theologiae Mysti-co-Scholasticae,* new ed., 6 vols. (Bruges, Belgium: Carolum Beyaert,

For modern audiences, subtle debates over the nature and possibility of acquired contemplation, for example, seemed to pale in comparison with the more direct and personal appeal of Thérèse of Lisieux and a host of twentieth-century Carmelite saints, heroes, and teachers who followed.

Today we have come to recognize that Carmel is about much more than Teresa and John, as great as they may be, and about much more than cultivating one's private "spiritual life," understood in a narrow sense. Hence the Center's focus on the wider Carmelite tradition rather than exclusively on its "spirituality." Indeed, "Carmelites typically do not distinguish their spirituality from their whole way of life, and no simple description can capture all the rich diversity of its symbols, themes, practices, and representative figures."[5]

A Broader Perspective

As Professor Egan ably explains in his lecture, the Carmelite tradition is a Christian movement with a history of over 800 years, and a sense of self-identity that reaches back even further to the biblical figures of Mary and Elijah. Unlike the other three classic mendicant Orders that take their names from a foundational figure (Franciscans, Dominicans, Augustinians), the Carmelites take their name from the *place* where they began, a range of hills in northern Israel full of biblical resonances. Mount Carmel, of course, is forever associated with the prophet Elijah,

---

1925). See also, for example, Efrén de la Madre de Dios and Otger Steggink, s.v., "Carmelite Spirituality," in *New Catholic Encyclopedia,* ed. William J. McDonald, et al (New York: McGraw-Hill, 1967), 117; McGinn, *Mysticism in the Golden Age of Spain (1500–1650),* 377–78.

5   Steven Payne, *The Carmelite Tradition* (Collegeville, Minn.: Liturgical Press, 2011), xiii–xiv.

revered by Christians, Jews, and Muslims alike. It was here that he had his dramatic confrontation with the prophets of Baal (1 Kgs 18:19–40) and where his servant saw the small cloud signaling the end of the long drought (1 Kgs 18:42–46). It was here as well, according to modern historians, that a group of anonymous Western hermits gathered in the *wadi 'ain es-Siāh* around the end of the twelfth century, "iuxta fontem in Monte Carmeli," that is, near what was known as the "spring of Elijah" on Mount Carmel, dedicating themselves to prayer and solitude, but in a loose-knit community structure. As Egan notes, some time between 1206 and 1214 they approached the Latin Patriarch of Jerusalem, Albert Avogadro of Vercelli for a "formula of life" (*formula vitae*) in keeping with their "avowed purpose" (*propositum*) and particular manner of living "in allegiance to Jesus Christ" (*in obsequio Iesu Christi*).[6]

The text he provided—as later amended by Innocent IV—became known as the Carmelite Rule, the foundational document for a new family in the church and all that it would later become, as well as all that it would later contribute. Though brief, the Carmelite Rule stresses a number of elements:

- fraternal life and an authority of service (with a prior rather than an abbot)
- fasting and abstinence
- clothing oneself in the "armor" of the virtues
- work
- silence
- discretion

---

6 The text of the Carmelite Rule can be found in Payne, *The Carmelite Tradition*, 5–9. Inline references use the modern paragraph numbering agreed upon by the Carmelite and Discalced Carmelite general administrations.

- recitation of the Divine Office or its equivalent
- daily Eucharist together (when possible) in the oratory to be constructed in the midst of their hermitages
- and, most memorably, solitary prayer "in one's cell meditating on the Law of the Lord day and night" (*Rule,* 10).

Centuries later, Teresa of Ávila, like so many others in the Carmelite tradition, would identify this "unceasing prayer" as "the most important aspect of the rule" (W 4.2) and would explain it not so much in terms of reciting endless prayers but in terms of "an intimate sharing between friends; . . . taking time frequently to be alone with Him who we know loves us" (L 8.5).[7]

The location itself gave rise to the conviction among the Carmelites of being somehow deeply linked to the Old Testament prophets and inheritors of the Elijan spirit, though the interpretation of this prophetic dimension has certainly evolved over time. Likewise, the oratory that the original hermits built according to Albert's directive (*Rule,* 14) became even more decisive for their self-understanding because they dedicated it to Mary, thus recognizing her as the "lady of the place" and model of their vocation—their protector, mother, and even sister. Eventually

---

7   All English translations of Teresa's texts are from *The Collected Works of St. Teresa of Avila,* 3 vols., trans. Kieran Kavanaugh and Otilio Rodriguez (Washington, D.C.: ICS Publications, 1976–1986). Abbreviations for Teresa's major works are as follows: F = *Book of Foundations;* IC = *Interior Castle*; L = *Book of Her Life*; W = *Way of Perfection*. For the *Foundations, Life,* and *Way of Perfection,* the first number refers to the chapter and the second to the paragraph. For the *Interior Castle,* the first number refers to the "dwelling place," the second to the chapter, and the third to the paragraph. Thus "L 1.2" refers to the second paragraph of the first chapter in the *Life,* while "IC 6.5.4" refers to the fourth paragraph in chapter 5 of the sixth dwelling place in the *Interior Castle.*

it gave rise to the name by which they came to be known, the brothers of Our Lady of Mount Carmel, and the recognition of the Carmelites as a pre-eminently Marian order.

With the political situation deteriorating in Palestine, the Carmelites returned to Europe and gradually adapted themselves to the mendicant life, yet keeping alive the "dangerous memory"[8] of the original hermit community on Mount Carmel. As the Order grew and spread, then, it came to represent far more than a certain rarified mysticism of the spiritually elite. The Carmelites have had their famous ascetics, mystics, and solitaries, to be sure, but they have also had great artists, like Filippo Lippi (who was apparently a better painter than friar); skilled poets like Baptist of Mantua, John of the Cross, and Jessica Powers; military heroes like Nuno Álvares Pereira—the liberator of Portugal—or Georges Thierry d'Argenlieu (Louis of the Trinity)—a commanding officer of the Free French Naval Forces during World War II; great churchmen and ecclesiastical diplomats like Saint Peter-Thomas— Latin Patriarch of Constantinople in the fourteenth century—or Bishop Donal Lamont in twentieth century Africa; great servants of the poor, sick, and elderly, like the recently beatified Angelo Paoli and the founders and members of many of the "active" Carmelite congregations of women; notable martyrs like Titus Brandsma and Edith Stein—who died in the Nazi death camps—

---

8   This term is borrowed from Metz, who distinguishes false soothing nostalgia for a past golden age from the subversive power of a "remembered history of suffering" and freedom, especially exemplified in the *anamnesis* of the passion, death, and resurrection of Christ. See Johann Baptist Metz, *Faith in History and Society: Toward a Practical Fundamental Theology,* trans. David Smith (New York: Crossroad Book, Seabury Press, 1980), 109–10, 195–96. Analogously, over the past eight centuries the "remembering" of Carmel's origins has repeatedly served as a challenge to the status quo and opened up fresh possibilities for the future.

or the nuns of Compiègne, guillotined during the Reign of Terror, whose story has become so widely known through the modern opera *Dialogues of the Carmelites*; outstanding scholars like John Baconthorpe in the medieval period, the aforementioned Titus Brandsma and Edith Stein in the first half of the twentieth century, and the Scripture scholar Roland Murphy and the great Mariologist Eamon Carroll, who walked the corridors of Catholic University's Caldwell Hall within living memory.[9] Among the best-known Catholic popular devotions are the Brown Scapular, the Infant of Prague, and the Holy Face, though devotees may not realize that they have their historical roots in Carmel, nor that the Carmelites also played a key role in promoting devotion to Saint Joseph. Today the "vine of Carmel" has a profusion of branches, including the Order of Carmelites and Order of Discalced Carmelites (with their friars, nuns, and lay members), as well as scores of aggregated congregations, secular institutes, ecclesial movements, and so on.

Indeed, given this rich history, we might say that there are many "Carmelite traditions" and many ways to be Carmelite. And yet:

Down through the ages, these varied Carmelite expressions have returned again and again to certain images, themes, and spiritual models in pondering the mystery of divine-human friendship: the mountain, the garden, the spring, the hermit's cell, the journey, night, fire, the heart, allegiance to Jesus Christ, continual pondering of

---

9   The Carmelite tradition even includes famous "black sheep," like the Anglican ex-Carmelite John Bale (1495–1563), who wrote the *Summary of the Famous Writers of Great Britain,* or Père Hyacinthe Loyson (1827–1912), the Discalced Carmelite who was excommunicated for his unorthodox preaching and whose case became a focus of St. Thérèse's prayerful concern.

the Law of the Lord, radical availability to God [*vacare Deo*], mystical union, self-transcending love, contemplative prayer, prophetic zeal, Elijah, Mary, Joseph, and so on.[10]

Of course, nothing on this list is unique to Carmel, which is, after all, just one of the "many and varied" ways of living "a life of allegiance to Jesus Christ" (*Rule,* 2). Carmelites have learned much from other traditions. Nevertheless, the Carmelite tradition has its own particular way of putting together these constitutive elements. And the common thread, if I may hazard a great oversimplification of my own, is a radical thirst for the divine, or as the classic medieval Carmelite text *The Book of the Institution of the First Monks* puts it: "to taste somewhat in the heart and to experience in the mind the power of the divine presence and the sweetness of heavenly glory, not only after death but already in this mortal life."[11] Edith Stein writes that the Carmelite vocation is "to stand before the face of the living God" like Elijah,[12] and Titus Brandsma agrees that "this living in the presence of God ... is a characteristic which the children of Carmel have inherited from the great Prophet."[13] For Carmelites, the ever-deepening contemplative encounter with the triune God at the heart of their vocation leads to a loving union that is totally transformative—or as John of the Cross puts it, "divinizing"—so that one becomes "by participation" what Christ is "by nature,"

---

10   Payne, *The Carmelite Tradition,* xiv.

11   See the excerpt in Payne, *The Carmelite Tradition,* 24–25.

12   Edith Stein, "On the History and Spirit of Carmel," in *The Hidden Life: Hagiographic Essays, Meditations, Spiritual Texts,* trans. Waltraut Stein, ed. Lucy Gelber and Michael Linssen (Washington, D.C.: ICS Publications, 1992), 1.

13   Titus Brandsma, *Carmelite Mysticism: Historical Sketches* (Chicago: Carmelite Press, 1936), 12.

through a sharing in God's own life, knowledge, and love.[14] As a result, those who faithfully follow the Carmelite path cannot help but become enflamed at the same time with a zealous love for their brothers and sisters, and for all creation, because one cannot be truly conformed to God without sharing God's love for all creatures.

Carmelite Studies

Anyone asking Carmelites a century ago about the meaning of the expression "Carmelite Studies" would likely have been met with a blank stare, as that terminology was not used in academic or popular writings at the time. Even the narrower notion of "Carmelite spirituality," as something distinct from other spiritualities, was only just beginning to emerge. Actually, the recently canonized (May 15, 2022) Dutch Carmelite scholar and martyr Titus Brandsma was one of the first to attempt a kind of modern synthetic overview when he wrote the article on the Carmelite spirituality of the Ancient Observance for the

---

14   See, for example, N 2.6.1; C 22.3, 27.7, 36.5, 39.4-6; F 1.29. All English-language quotations of John's writings are taken from *The Collected Works of St. John of the Cross*, rev. ed., trans. Kieran Kavanaugh and Otilio Rodriguez (Washington, D.C.: ICS Publications, 1991). Abbreviations for John's prose texts are as follows: A = *Ascent of Mount Carmel*; C = *Spiritual Canticle*; F = *Living Flame of Love*; N = *Dark Night;* Sayings = *Sayings of Light and Love*. In references to both *The Ascent* and *The Dark Night*, the first number indicates the book, the second number refers to the chapter, and the third number refers to the paragraph. For example, "A 2.3.4" refers to book two, chapter 3, paragraph 4 of *The Ascent*. Similarly, for *The Spiritual Canticle* and *The Living Flame of Love*, the first number refers to the stanza and the second number to the paragraph. Thus, "C 3.4" is a reference to stanza 3, paragraph 4 of *The Spiritual Canticle* commentary.

famous multivolume *Dictionnaire de spiritualité* published in the 1930s.

To be sure, there were important and influential collections of documents on the history and heritage of the Carmelites even in the Middle Ages, just as there were for other orders and congregations. Moreover, Carmel has a long history of important scholarship and major scholars.[15] We have even produced three doctors of the church, including one who has been called "the greatest saint of modern times."[16] And though we no longer claim a literal founding by the prophet Elijah, which would have made us the oldest religious order in the church by far, we can certainly claim an enormously rich 800-year intellectual, cultural, and spiritual legacy.

Still, if I am not mistaken, the idea of recognizing a particular religious order's broad heritage as constituting its own field of interdisciplinary academic and pastoral study is of relatively recent origin. Here in the United States one thinks of the Franciscan Institute, founded around 1940 at St. Bonaventure's College in upstate New York; or the Institute of Cistercian Studies founded in 1973 (which has become the Center for Cistercian and Monastic Studies of the Medieval Institute at Western Michigan University in Kalamazoo); or the more recent Institute for Advanced Jesuit Studies inaugurated at Boston College in 2014. Thus, today there are a number of similar examples of study and research centers organized around a particular religious charism.

---

15   In addition to medieval theologians like John Baconthorpe, early modern scholastics like the celebrated Discalced Carmelites of Salamanca, and the aforementioned martyred scholars Titus Brandsma and Edith Stein, there have been many twentieth/twenty-first-century Carmelite scholars who have taught at some point at The Catholic University of America: Christian Ceroke, Romaeus O'Brien, Ernest Larkin, Kieran Kavanaugh, John Sullivan, Eamon Carroll, Roland Murphy, Quinn Conner, and Leopold Glueckert.

16   Attributed to Pius X, and often seconded by others.

Within the Carmelite family as well, this interest in a deeper understanding and scholarly study of our own particular heritage has been growing over the last several decades. On the side of the Ancient Observance, for instance, there is the Institutum Carmelitanum in Rome, established in 1951 by the Carmelite Prior General Kilian Lynch to promote studies in Carmelite history, Mariology, and spirituality; there is the Titus Brandsma Instituut in the Netherlands, jointly founded by the Dutch Carmelite Province and the University of Nijmegen (now Radboud University); and numerous other examples, not forgetting the wonderful Carmelitana Collection at Whitefriars Hall near the Catholic University of America, one of the best library resources for Carmelite research in the world. On the Discalced side there is the scholarly work in the Carmelite tradition associated with the Pontifical Faculty "Teresianum" in Rome and the Centro Internacional Teresiano-Sanjuanista in Ávila, as well as the "Institute of Carmelite Studies" in Washington, D.C., which, among other things, has provided affordable and reliable editions of many Carmelite classics in contemporary American English. In addition—and particularly important as a model for future teamwork—there are the *collaborative* efforts among the different branches of the Carmelite family, both female and male, including the Carmelite Forum which for many years organized major summer seminars in the Carmelite tradition at Saint Mary's College in Notre Dame, Indiana; the Carmelite Institute of Britain and Ireland, which has provided online courses accredited through St. Patrick's College, Maynooth; and the Carmelite Institute of North America, which offers a variety of scholarly resources.

What all of these initiatives have in common, I would suggest, is the burning conviction that the patrimony (and "*matri*-mony") of the great religious families in general—and Carmel in particular—offers a vast treasury of profound knowledge, varied cultural expressions, and practical wisdom that is in danger of being lost because of the declining numbers of those professionally trained to explore them. There is an urgent and ongoing need for the rigorous scholarship that Professor Egan's work exemplifies and which his lecture calls for so eloquently. Borrowing an image from John of the Cross, we might compare the Carmelite tradition to "an abundant mine with many recesses of treasures, so that however deep individuals may go they never reach the end or bottom, but rather in every recess find new veins with new riches everywhere" (C 37.4).[17] Borrowing a page from the Commission on the Franciscan Intellectual Tradition (CFIT), we can say that Carmel also has its own vital "'word' to speak to people today," one that arises out of its fundamental commitment to prayer and contemplation and "responds to deeply-felt needs in our Church and our world."[18]

Contemporary Contributions

What does this lively 800-year-old tradition have to offer to our church and world today? Obviously not every potential contribution can be mentioned here. Still less am I claiming that Carmelites are the *only* ones who can make these contributions. But here, briefly, are a few that may prove to be particularly significant.

First, Carmel is already playing a role in the ongoing rapprochement between spirituality and the academic discipline of theology. The theologian Mark McIntosh has written that "the mystic and the theologian are always being led to a perception of the same mysteries, only from different perspectives. More than this, the very patterns of their respective vocations lead

---

17 John of the Cross, *The Collected Works*, 615–26.
18 Quoted phrases are taken from the "About" page on the website of the Commission on the Franciscan Intellectual-Spiritual Tradition (CFIT), https://www.franciscantradition.org/about-us.

them towards convergence if never quite identity."[19] David Tracy has argued that "a mystical element affects all three of the major types of theology: fundamental, systematic and practical. Fundamental theology's crucial notion of reason is deepened by mystical contemplation and apophasis. Systematic theology's naming of God as Infinite Trinitarian Love is deepened by a mysticism of infinity, love, and Trinity. Practical theology is strengthened by explicit attention to the prophetical-mystical character."[20] Carmelite mystics and spiritual writers are among those most often cited in such discussions. Thus theologians are already mining the texts of Teresa and John of the Cross for fresh insights into Christology and the theology of faith and revelation,[21] or exploring Thérèse of Lisieux's eschatology and "ecclesiology of love,"[22] or examining Elizabeth of the Trinity's perspectives on the divine indwelling of the triune God. It stands to reason that contemplatives who seek to enter more deeply into "the thicket of God's wisdom and knowledge," as John of the Cross describes it, and to "know them from further within" (see C 36.10–11) might offer valuable perspectives to those who study these same mysteries through the academic discipline of theology.

Second, though Teresa of Ávila and John of the Cross are sometimes "blamed" for encouraging the trend toward an overly

---

19 Mark McIntosh, *Mystical Theology: The Integrity of Spirituality and Theology* (Malden, Mass.: Blackwell Publishers, 1998), 33.

20 See the abstract for David Tracy, "Theology and Mysticism," a talk delivered at "Mysticism and Contemporary Life: A Conference in Honor of Bernard McGinn," held at the Oblate School of Theology in San Antonio, Tex., on October 12–13, 2018. See https://www.youtube.com/watch?v=qDu6dlfLLt0.

21 Iain Matthew, "Visualising Christology: Llama de amor viva and the Resurrection," *Teresianum* 68, no. 1 (2017): 87–125.

22 William Thompson, *Fire and Light: The Saints and Theology: On Consulting the Saints, Mystics, and Martyrs in Theology* (Mahwah, N.J.: Paulist Press, 1987), 171–77.

psychological approach to mysticism and spirituality, many authors today are creatively applying their analyses of particular stages in the individual's journey to society as a whole. Constance FitzGerald and others have extended John of the Cross's famous treatment of the "dark night" to contemporary social experiences of darkness and impasse.[23] As Pope Saint John Paul II has written, "Our age has known times of anguish which have made us understand this expression better and which have furthermore given it a kind of collective character . . . . The term *dark night* is now used of all of life and not just of a phase of the spiritual journey. The Saint's doctrine is now invoked in response to this unfathomable mystery of human suffering."[24] More generally, the Carmelite tradition offers reliable guidance for times when the old certainties and familiar guideposts seem to crumble. Though I am hardly unbiased, it seems to me that no other tradition more fully explores the radical depths of the individual and collective purification we need, just as no other tradition is more optimistic about the ultimate goal of the purification process.

Third, though the record is certainly mixed, I would suggest that the Carmelite tradition—like other traditions associated with the older religious orders—has often provided an important space for the unfolding and expression of women's experience and

---

23 See, for example, Constance FitzGerald, "From Impasse to Prophetic Hope: Crisis of Memory," *Proceedings of the Catholic Theological Society of America* 64 (2009): 21–42; Constance FitzGerald, "Impasse and Dark Night," in *Living with Apocalypse: Spiritual Resources for Social Compassion*, ed. Tilden Edwards (San Francisco: Harper & Row, 1984), 93–116; Laurie Cassidy and M. Shawn Copeland, eds., *Desire, Darkness, and Hope: Theology in a Time of Impasse: Engaging the Thought of Constance FitzGerald, OCD* (Collegeville, Minn.: Liturgical Press, 2021).

24 John Paul II, "Master in the Faith: Apostolic Letter for the Fourth Centenary of the Death of Saint John of the Cross," *L'Osservatore Romano* 52, no. 14, English ed. (December 24, 1990), 8.

spirituality. The influence of Teresa of Ávila's *Book of Her Life* and other works, for example, inspired generations of Carmelite women who followed in her literary footsteps. We owe a debt of gratitude to scholars in the field of women's studies who have retrieved many of these women's long-ignored texts and shown their contemporary relevance. More than just collections of personal anecdotes or catalogues of private ecstasies and visions, these texts show how these women of the past claimed their own voice and engaged in a genuine "vernacular theology" (to use a term from medieval studies).[25]

Fourth, though it is not widely known today, Carmelites have played a key role not only in the church's missions but in the development of missiology itself. In the seventeenth century, for example, Thomas of Jesus (Dávila) wrote one of the earliest and most influential missiological treatises, *De procuranda salute omnium gentium.* Peter of the Mother of God (Villagrasa) and Dominic of Jesus and Mary (Ruzzola) were successively appointed

---

25   See, for example, Electa Arenal and Stacey Schlau, *Untold Sisters: Hispanic Nuns in Their Own Works* (Albuquerque, N.Mex.: University of New Mexico Press, 1989); Julián Urkiza, ed., *Obras Completas de la Beata Ana de San Bartolomé,* 2 vols., (Rome: Edizioni Teresianum, 1985); Ana de San Bartolomé, *Autobiography and Other Writings,* trans. Darcy Donohue, The Other Voice in Early Modern Europe Series (Chicago: University of Chicago Press, 2008); Elizabeth Teresa Howe, *The Visionary Life of Madre Ana de San Agustín* (Woodbridge, Suffolk: Tamesis, 2004); María de San José Salazar, *Book for the Hour of Recreation,* trans. Alison Weber (Chicago: University of Chicago Press, 2002); Cecilia de Nacimiento, *Obras Completas,* ed. José M. Diaz Ceron (Madrid: Editorial de Espiritualidad, 1971); Cecilia de Nacimiento, *Journeys of a Mystical Soul in Poetry and Prose,* ed. Kevin Donnelly and Sandra Sider (Toronto: Centre for Reformation and Renaissance Studies, 2012). "Vernacular theology" is typically used to refer to an often neglected third stream of medieval theology, alongside scholastic and monastic theology.

"Superintendents of the Missions" by the pope and—along with Jerome Gracian—helped promote the establishment of the Congregation for the Propagation of the Faith, now known as the Dicastery for Evangelization.[26] And it is no accident that a Carmelite nun, Thérèse of Lisieux, was named co-patron of the missions in 1927, not because of pressure from Carmelites but at the request of the missionaries themselves. In this respect, Thérèse is a faithful daughter of her spiritual mother, Teresa of Ávila, who is often credited as one of the first founders of contemplative congregations to recognize the essentially apostolic purpose of the contemplative life. Of course, Carmelites struggle like everyone else to balance times of prayer with other obligations. But we recognize that the contemplative and prophetic elements of the charism are not in conflict and not just arbitrarily and uneasily joined together, but that we are apostolic and prophetic precisely *because* we are contemplative. All of this has important implications for the theology and practice of the new evangelization.

Fifth, the traditional Carmelite commitment to extended periods of meditation and contemplative prayer has caught the attention of researchers in the newly developing field of "neuro-theology," which studies the correlation between religious and spiritual activities and experiences and neural activity in the brain. For example, one famous and much-discussed Canadian study on whether there exists a particular "God spot" in the brain was based on MRI data collected from Carmelite nuns.[27] On the other hand,

---

26 See Florencio del Niño Jesús, *La Orden de Santa Teresa, la Fundación de la Propaganda Fidei, y las Misiones Carmelitanas* (Madrid: Nieto y Compañía, 1923); Elisée Alford, *Les missions des Carmes Déchaux, 1575–1975,* Présence du Carmel 13 (Paris: Desclée de Brouwer, 1977), 25–31; Peter-Thomas Rohrbach, *Journey to Carith* (New York: Doubleday & Co., 1966), 233–34.

27 See Mario Beauregard, "Neural Correlates of a Mystical Experience in Carmelite Nuns," *Neuroscience Letters* 405 (September 25, 2006):

much of the current scientific research seems to equate meditation with practices rooted in Hinduism and Buddhism, such as TM or "mindfulness" exercises, while generally ignoring traditional Western meditative practices. Perhaps Carmelites would make good research subjects. But perhaps also the Carmelite tradition can assist these researchers in clarifying their philosophical and theological presuppositions, which often seem somewhat limited, reductive, or confused.

Sixth, we should not forget Carmel's long and fruitful association with the creative arts in all their rich variety. As noted earlier, for eight centuries the Carmelite family has produced numerous painters, poets, musicians, and other artists, from Fra Lippo Lippi to Jessica Powers. Moreover, the saints and heroes of Carmel have inspired countless novelists, composers, playwrights, and filmmakers. The Center will want to be attentive to these many and varied ways of communicating the wisdom and beauty arising out of the Carmelite encounter with the living God.

Finally, the Carmelite tradition is an important meeting point for ecumenical and interfaith dialogue, especially the "spiritual ecumenism" which Vatican II described as "the soul of the whole ecumenical movement"[28] (and others have called "the inescapable way forward").[29] Though I am not an expert in this area, I am often struck by the way that Carmelite saints and

---

186–90; Helen Pearson, "Nuns Go under the Brain Scanner," *Nature* (August 30, 2006), https://www.nature.com/news/2006/060828/full/060828-3.html; "Doubt Cast Over Brain 'God Spot'," *BBC News* (August 30, 2006), http://news.bbc.co.uk/2/hi/health/5296728.stm.

28 Vatican Council II, *Unitatis Redintegratio* (November 21, 1964), 8; available at www.vatican.va.

29 See Brian Farrell, "Spiritual Ecumenism: The Inescapable Way Forward," *People on the Move* 97 suppl. (April 2005); available at www.vatican.va.

texts are able to cross denominational boundaries. A statue of Teresa of Ávila, for example, can be found in the Washington National Cathedral (Episcopalian), and the former archbishop of Canterbury, Rowan Williams, has written extensively on Carmelite saints.[30] Brother Lawrence's *Practice of the Presence of God* is enormously popular even among Protestant groups that are normally skeptical of Catholic spirituality. The Edith Stein Guild in New York promotes dialogue between Christians and Jews. Muslim women frequently come to pray in the shrine of St. Thérèse in Cairo, Egypt. Hindus and Buddhists (and even atheists) study the works of John of the Cross. The Carmelite basilica of Stella Maris on Mount Carmel is a pilgrimage destination for Christians, Muslims, Jews, and even members of the Bahá'í faith. Professor Michael Root of Catholic University's School of Theology and Religious Studies has recently argued for a "normal ecumenism" that "would seek less to achieve decisive breakthroughs than to deepen the real but limited communion that exists already."[31] Without ignoring our seemingly intractable theological and religious differences, we should not neglect our deeper common yearning for the Transcendent, our desire to stand together before the face of the living God.

Perhaps the Carmelite tradition may even help alleviate in some way the deepening polarization affecting the contemporary church and society, with our steady stream of scandals and distractions, and with each of us cocooned in our social media bubbles and ideological echo chambers. Here, too, Carmelite saints and texts are valued across the political and religious spectrum by those who agree on little else. In the midst of so many shrill and

---

30 Both Teresa and John of the Cross appear in the liturgical calendar of the Episcopal Church in the United States; see *A Great Cloud of Witnesses: A Calendar of Commemorations* (New York: Church Publishing, 2016).

31 Michael Root, "Ecumenical Winter," *First Things* 286 (October 2018), 38.

conflicting voices, the Carmelite tradition can teach us how to turn off the cell phones, turn down noise, learn how to recollect ourselves, ponder the Word of God in the silence of our hearts, and allow the Spirit to purify us of all our hidden preconceptions and prejudices so that we can really listen and speak to one another with love and respect, recognizing (as Edith Stein puts it) that those who seek the Truth are seeking God, whether they realize it or not.

Conclusion

What, then, will the Center for Carmelite Studies be doing to realize these goals and share these riches? Put simply, we will be promoting scholarly studies and research in the Carmelite tradition, which encompasses far more than its spirituality, as valuable as that may be. We expect to provide a range of academic programs and awards—both on campus and virtually—while offering academic guidance and financial support to those studying under the Center's auspices. In addition to the Annual Lecture in Carmelite Studies, we are organizing other public lectures, seminars, and workshops, as well as interdisciplinary conferences on topics of shared interest with other academic centers, both within and beyond Catholic University. In collaboration with Catholic University of America Press, we hope to promote the publication of scholarly monographs, articles, and reviews, such as the volume you now hold in your hands. There will be opportunities to collaborate with those in the fields of church history, systematic and historical theology, biblical and pastoral studies, missiology, moral theology, Catholic social teaching and outreach, religion and culture, ecumenism and inter-faith dialogue, and many other areas in which Carmel has an important contribution to make. We will "network" with the many different centers and initiatives in the field of Carmelite studies around the world, so that we can collaborate rather than duplicate or compete with what they are doing. And while striving for all of this, we will make sure that more pastorally-oriented Carmelite programs are not neglected.

Great Carmelite scholars such as Professor Keith J. Egan, the first presenter in our "Annual Lecture in Carmelite Studies" series, are already pointing the way forward, as the following pages show. Our hope is that this initiative will become known as an outstanding and truly global "center" for relevant contemporary study and research in the Carmelite tradition, which is such a vital resource for meeting the challenges of our time. And we are grateful that it is finding its home in the School of Theology and Religious Studies at the heart of The Catholic University of America, which trains lay and ordained leadership for every level of the church and society today and continues to be engaged in the great theological and social conversations of our times. May God bless the work before us!

Steven Payne, OCD
Endowed Chair of Carmelite Studies
Center for Carmelite Studies
The Catholic University of America

"WHAT MAKES
A CARMELITE A CARMELITE?"
EXPLORING CARMEL'S CHARISM

As the thirteenth century got underway two important institutions came into existence—the university and the mendicant orders—which have interacted with one another ever since. A fruit of this relationship between a university and the Carmelite

*   I am grateful to Father Steven Payne, OCD, the first holder of the Endowed Chair in Carmelite Studies at The Catholic University of America and to Brother Daryl Moresco, O. Carm., director of the Center for Carmelite Studies at the same university, for the invitation to deliver the inaugural lecture in a series known as "The Annual Lecture in Carmelite Studies at The Catholic University of America." I owe special thanks to Patrick Mullins, O. Carm., whose scholarship has been so helpful for this lecture, especially his *St Albert of Jerusalem and the Roots of Carmelite Spirituality* (Rome: Edizioni Carmelitane, 2012).

23

Order is the Endowed Chair and Center for Carmelite Studies at The Catholic University of America.[1] A generous gift to the university by the Carmelite Province of the Most Pure Heart of Mary has been reciprocated by the warm hospitality extended by the university to Carmel. The Endowed Chair and Center are unique gifts to all who cherish Carmel's wisdom, a wisdom for all who seek guidance about prayer and the possibility of contemplation.

I dedicate this essay to the eminent historian and poet of the Carmelite Order, Father Joachim Smet (1915–2011)[2] and to Carmelites everywhere. I have been enriched beyond measure by the Carmelite Family of nuns, sisters, friars, and fellow lay Carmelites. As Assistant General of the Carmelite Order, Father Smet arranged, albeit without my knowledge, that I be assigned to study under Dom David Knowles, OSB (d. 1974), at Cambridge University, England. Knowles was an acclaimed expert on monasticism and mysticism. Dom David had a special interest and fondness for Teresa of Jesus and John of the Cross.[3] In his last letter to me before he died, Dom David wrote: "I am surer than ever that prayer (of the heart & soul) is the first work of a religious—prayer that is love." Dom David's sentiment is germane to the theme of this essay, Carmel's charism.[4] If a reader belongs to a tradition other than Carmel, the main thrust of this paper is applicable to them and to other traditions like the Benedictines,

---

1   Originally the Carmelite Order was an eremitic community before it became a mendicant order. The focus of this lecture is on Carmel's original eremitic era.

2   Keith J. Egan, "Obituary: Joachim F. Smet, O. Carm. (1915–2011)," *The Catholic Historical Review* 98, no. 1 (2012): 196–98.

3   Keith J. Egan, "Dom David Knowles, 1896–1974," *The Benedictine Review* 27, no. 3 (1976): 235–46; and Egan, "Dom David Knowles," *The New Catholic Encyclopedia*, 2nd ed., vol. 17 (1978).

4   Letter from David Knowles to Keith J. Egan, June 22, 1974.

Dominicans, Franciscans, and the Augustinian Friars; in fact, all Christians have a stake in the charisms of the Holy Spirit.

This is not the first time that I have explored Carmelite identity. In 1978 I was invited to join a small group of scholars who met during a conference at York University in Toronto on the theme "Consciousness and Group Identification in High Medieval Religion." My lecture was entitled: "The Search for Identity by Medieval Carmelites, 1200–1326."[5] The group consisted of the Dominican Leonard Boyle, the Benedictine Dom Jean Leclercq, Professors Giles Constable, Bernard McGinn, Caroline Walker Bynum, Richard Schneider, and myself. At that time my search for historical data about Carmelite identity was disappointing. Sources for my topic were in short supply. Many of Carmel's medieval texts were unidentified, unedited, or unexplored. Forty-three years later the story is different. Numerous sources are available, expertly edited, and professionally explored by Carmelite scholars too numerous to list here, but these scholars have made possible responses to the questions: What makes a Carmelite a Carmelite? And what does it mean for associated members of the Carmelite Family to participate in the Carmelite charism?

---

5   This lecture has not been published but is available from the author upon request. On Carmelite identity see Richard Copsey, "Establishment, Identity and Papal Approval: The Carmelite Order's Creation of Its Legendary History," *Carmelus* 47 (2000): 41–53, reprinted in *Carmel in Britain* 3 (Faversham, Kent, UK: Saint Albert's Press and Rome: Edizioni Carmelitane, 2004), 1–15; Jens Röhrkasten and Coralie Zermatten, eds., *Historiography and Identity: Responses to Medieval Carmelite Culture* (Vienna: LIT Verlag, 2017). On the Carmelite Family, see *Johan Bergström-Allen, ed., Climbing the Mountain: The Carmelite Journey* (Faversham, Kent, UK: Saint Albert's Press, 2010).

The Second Vatican Council

Vatican II was the most significant religious event of the twentieth century; its teachings included a presentation of Catholic doctrine regarding the consecrated or religious life. On October 28, 1965, twelve days before the council concluded its deliberations, Pope Saint Paul VI promulgated the decree *Perfectae caritatis* (Of Perfect Love). 'Perfect' here is not to be taken in the sense that something is without imperfection; rather one is perfect when one becomes what one can become with God's help. This decree directed religious communities to undertake "an up-to-date renewal of the religious life [that] comprises both a constant return to the sources of Christian life in general and to the primitive inspiration of the institutes, and their adaptation to the changed conditions of our time."[6] The council and its aftermath sent religious to explore the sources of their identity. Religious communities became adept at reading the signs of the times.[7] Since then, untold hours of research, countless meetings, books, and articles have ensued as religious communities across the globe explored their identity. Like other orders and congregations, Carmelites have now spent more than five decades since Vatican II on a communal search for their historical identity and on a mission to discern their charism.[8]

---

6   Decree on the Up-to-date Renewal of Religious Life *Perfectae caritatis*, no. 2. In *Vatican Council II: Constitutions, Decrees, Declarations*, ed. Austin Flannery (Northport, N.Y.: Costello Publishing, 1996).

7   Cf. Mt 16:4. Pope Saint John XXIII used the biblical phrase, "signs of the times," in his Apostolic Constitution *Humanae salutis*. In *Acta Apostolicae Sedis* 54 (1962), 5–13.

     An English translation can be found at https://jakomonchak.files. wordpress.com/2011/12/humanae-salutis.pdf, accessed on April 13, 2021.

8   Sandra M. Schneiders, "Foreword," in Loan Le, *Religious Life: A Reflective Examination of Its Charism and Mission for Today* (Newcastle upon Tyne: Cambridge Scholars, 2016), vii–x.

Historical Identity and Charism as Partners

Saint Teresa of Ávila could be loquacious, yet she could also be quite concise. This first female doctor of the church described the Carmelite charism in a nutshell: "all of us who wear this holy habit of Carmel are called to prayer and contemplation."[9] Carmel's charism includes more than prayer and contemplation; yet nothing is more important to a Carmelite than prayer and contemplation. In 2002 Carmelites celebrated the 550th anniversary of the papal document *Cum nulla* which for the first-time welcomed women as full-fledged members of the Carmelite Order and which approved the existence of the Carmelite Third Order. At the time of that anniversary Saint John Paul II, who had a unique affinity for Carmel, wrote: "Carmel [is] where prayer becomes life and life flourishes in prayer."[10] No matter how concisely one crafts a statement about the Carmelite charism, prayer and contemplation can never be omitted since they are at the heart of Carmel's original charism.

A sign of an authentic religious identity, whether personal or communal, is spiritual maturity. We live in an era intensely conscious of the search for identity, an era ushered in by Sigmund Freud and Carl Jung. Later the psychoanalyst Erik Erikson stressed that a mature identity is alive not inert, dynamic not static. I shall not enlist psychology as part of this search because I am not trained to do so. Yet, Erik Erikson and others have unearthed important aspects of the search for an authentic identity. For example, Erikson's questions are applicable to both historical research and to the discernment of an order's

---

9   *The Interior Castle* 5.1.2., *The Collected Works of St. Teresa of Avila*,
      vol. 2, trans. Kieran Kavanaugh and Otilio Rodriguez (Washington,
      D.C.: ICS Publications, 1980).

10   John Paul II, "Message for the 550th Anniversary of the Papal Bull,
      Cum nulla, to Joseph Chalmers, O. Carm., Prior General of the
      Carmelite Order," Vatican City, October 7, 2002.

charism. Erikson's questions are: What do I want to make of myself? and What do I have to work with?[11] From a Christian perspective, Erikson's first question is about freedom while his second question concerns gift/grace. Grace and freedom are fundamental to Christian and Carmelite identity, as we shall see. Another reason for not highlighting psychology is that during the first century of Carmel's existence, almost nothing is known about the personalities of the Carmelite hermits nor even about those who, later in the thirteenth century, were in the process of becoming mendicants. That lack is no excuse for a failure to explore whatever sources may throw light on the identity of the early Carmelite hermits. The struggle of the earliest Carmelites to live in "allegiance to Jesus Christ" is what the Carmelite Rule bade them to be: committed disciples of Jesus Christ.[12] Later in the Carmelite tradition John of the Cross says that the initial step in Carmelite discipleship is to "have [an] habitual desire to imitate Christ in all your deeds…and [to] behave in all events as he would."[13] The consultation of Carmelites of later centuries can bring helpful insights about the Carmelite charism of earlier eras.

My perspectives in this essay are historical and theological, necessarily historical because Carmelites have learned the hard way that they must work avidly to attain factual accuracy in the exploration of their identity. Contemporary society is awash with

---

11   Questions culled from Erik Erikson, *Identity: Youth and Crisis* (New York: W.W. Norton, 1968), and Erikson, *Childhood and Society*, 2nd ed. (New York: W. W. Norton, 1963).

12   *The Rule of Saint Albert*, ed. Hugh Clarke and Bede Edwards (Aylesford and Kensington: The Friars, 1973), 79. See Giles Constable, "The Ideal of the Imitation of Christ," in Constable, *Three Studies in Medieval Religious and Social Thought* (Cambridge: Cambridge University Press, 1995), 143–248.

13   John of the Cross, "The Ascent of Mount Carmel," *The Collected Works of St. John of the Cross*, trans. Kieran Kavanaugh and Otilio Rodriguez (Washington, D.C.: ICS Publications, 1991), 1.13.3.

wildly concocted fantasies that rob one of trust in the authority of church, society, and scholarship as well as trust in one another. Trust, then and now, makes it possible to live with serenity and hope. Carmelites for too long a time were addicted to the fantasy that their order had originated in the ninth century BC, claiming that their historical founder was the prophet, Elijah.[14] This claim emerged when, with no known founder, the Carmelite hermits and friars were confronted with the fame of founders like Benedict, Francis of Assisi, Clare of Assisi, and Dominic Guzmán. All the while Carmelites had to deal with the painful reality of anonymous beginnings. Carmel's response to this anonymity wove a mythic and legendary origin. The Dutch Carmelite scholar Victor Roefs commented on this anonymity of the earliest Carmelites: "The glory of the Franciscan order is its founder, St. Francis. The glory of the Dominican order is its founder, St. Dominic. The glory of the Carmelite order is its striking anonymity. This order, having developed from a small group of hermits on Carmel, is as obscure in its origin as in the seclusion and simplicity of the eremitical life."[15] Carmelites became uneasy about the anonymity of their origins. In the fourteenth century

---

14 Rudolf Hendriks, "La succession héréditaire (1280–1451)," in *Élie le Prophète*," 2: *Au Carmel dans le Jüdaïsme et l'Islam*, Les Études Carmélitaines 35 (Bruges: Desclée de Brouwer, 1956), 34–81 — Or: Rudolf Hendrinks, "La succession héréditaire," in *Élie le prophéte*, II, Les Études Carmélitaines (Bruges: Desclée de Brouwer, 1956); Jane Ackerman, *Elijah, Prophet of Carmel* (Washington, D.C.: ICS Publications, 2003); Kilian Healy, *Prophet of Fire* (Rome: Edizioni Carmelitane, 1990); Roland E. Murphy, "Elijah the Prophet," in *Experiencing Our Biblical Heritage* (Peabody, Mass.: Hendrickson Publishers, 2001), 25–62.

15 Victor Roefs, "The Earliest Evidence Concerning the Carmelite Order," trans. Sean O'Leary, *The Sword* 19 (1956): 244. This essay is a translation of Roefs' "De oudste getuigenissen omtrent de Carmel-telenorde," *Carmel* 1 (1948): 7–35.

Carmelites composed a web of literature dedicated in large measure to the claim that the prophet Elijah was their historical founder and that Mary, the mother of Jesus, had interacted with the Carmelites during her lifetime. Not a little of that literature is legendary and mythical.[16]

Wishful thinking or the lack of thinking eventually created problems once the false claims in Carmelite literature were challenged by the Bollandists, a Jesuit undertaking that was initiated in the seventeenth century. The Bollandists made a firm commitment to rigorous research into the lives of the saints. The remarkable achievement of the Bollandists is the *Acta Sanctorum* (*Acts of the Saints*).[17] The lives of the saints are arranged by their feast days as they occur month to month. For too long Carmelites failed to accept Bollandist scholarship, wasting time and energy on the claim that Elijah was their historical founder. Finally, during the second half of the twentieth century, Carmelite scholars by the rigor of their scholarship have made amends, albeit indirectly, for their mistreatment of the Bollandists who had exposed the untrustworthy character of Carmelite legends.[18]

---

16   Adrianus Staring, ed., *Medieval Carmelite Heritage: Early Reflections on the Nature of the Order* (Rome: Institutum Carmelitanum, 1989). For the medieval Carmelite Constitutions until 1625 see *Corpus Constitutionum Ordinis Fratrum Beatissimae Virginis Mariae de Monte Carmelo*, vol. 1, 1281–1456, ed. Edison Tinambunan and Emanuele Boaga (Rome: Edizioni Carmelitane, 2011) and vol. 2, 1456–1904, ed. Edison Tinambunan (Rome: Edizioni Carmelitane, 2016). On the Marian identity of the Carmelite Order see Christopher O'Donnell, "Maria nel Carmelo," *Dizionario Carmelitano,* ed. Emanuele Boaga and Luigi Borriello (Rome: Città Nuova, 2008); and John Welch, ed., *Carmel and Mary: Theology and History of a Devotion* (Washington, D.C.: Carmelite Institute, 2002).

17   See the *Acta Sanctorum* at the Digital Library, Villanova University, Philadelphia, Pa.

18   Joachim Smet, *The Mirror of Carmel* (Darien, Ill.: Carmelite Media,

For the last seven decades Carmelite scholars have imitated, with unflinching rigor, the scholarship of the Bollandists. Carmelites no longer think that Bollandist scholarship should be placed on an index.

Carmel, as an intentional faith community, must adhere to rigorous scholarship as it endeavors to articulate an authentic historical identity and reliable versions of its charism. The Christian identity of human persons is a deeply religious undertaking. For Christians, human existence has a divine origin and a divine destiny.[19] As a faith community Carmel must explore its identity not only historically but also theologically from the perspective of charism, always with the conviction that a charism presupposes rigorous historical scholarship and the realization that charism is the gifted presence of the Holy Spirit.

That religious orders and congregations articulate their identity as charism was first suggested by Vatican II's assertion that religious life is a divine gift. The council's "Dogmatic Constitution on the Church" says that religious life is "a divine gift which it has received from its Lord." The text goes on to say: "some Christians are called by God...so that they may enjoy a special gift of grace in the life of the church and may contribute, each in his own way, to its saving mission."[20] The council's "Decree on the Up-to-Date Renewal of Religious Life," says the following about the divine gift received by religious communities: "Amid such a great variety

---

2011), 434, 441, 514–16; David Knowles, "The Bollandists," *Great Historical Enterprises: History and Problems in Monastic History* (London: Thomas Nelson and Sons, 1963). The *Acta Sanctorum Database* contains the entire *AS* and is available on CD-Rom.

19 On divine origin see Joseph Wawrykow, "Creation," *The Westminster Handbook to Thomas Aquinas* (Louisville, Ky.: Westminster Knox Press, 2005), 29–32; on divine destiny see the entry "Viator," 165–67, and for both topics, see "Anthropology," 4–8.

20 Dogmatic Constitution on the Church, *Lumen gentium*, no. 43.

of gifts, [that is, of religious congregations and orders] all those who are called by God to the practice of the evangelical counsels, and who make faithful profession of them, bind themselves to the Lord in a special way." The decree continues: "Under the impulse of love, which the holy Spirit pours into their hearts (Rom 5:5) they live more and more for Christ and for his body, the church (see Col 1:24)."[21] The charism of religious communities usually appears in their constitutions. Constitutions are submitted to the Holy See for approval. This process recognizes the ecclesial character of the community's charism. Some clerical exempt religious communities approve changes in their constitutions through their general chapter(s).[22]

Charism: A Gift of the Holy Spirit

A charism is a gift of the Holy Spirit "for building up the body of Christ" (Eph 4:12).[23] Moreover, charisms reveal the "dynamic presence" of the Holy Spirit.[24] The charism of a religious community is not some inert thing, nor a recruiting slogan;

21   *Perfectae caritatis,* no. 1.

22   *Code of Canon Law* (Vatican City: Libreria Editrice Vaticana, 1983), canon 596.

23   All Scripture citations are taken from the New Revised Standard Version Catholic Edition, unless they occur within a quotation from another document. On the meaning and development of charism see Le, *Religious Life*, chapter 1. See also Robert L. Fastiggi, "Charism," *New Catholic Encyclopedia,* 2nd. ed., *Supplement*, vol. 3 (2010), 254–57. G. Foley, "Charisms in Religious Life," *New Catholic Encyclopedia*, 2nd ed., *Supplement*, vol. 3 (2010), 393–94.

24   On the dynamism of the Holy Spirit, see Tomáš Špidlík, *The Spirituality of the Christian East: A Systematic Handbook,* trans. Anthony P. Gythiel (Kalamazoo, Mich.: Cistercian Publications, 1986), 75–78; M. John Farrelly, "Holy Spirit," *The New Dictionary of Catholic Spirituality*, ed. Michael Downey (Collegeville, Minn.: Liturgical Press, 1993), 492–503, especially 496–99.

rather, a charism is the active and dynamic presence of the Holy Spirit within a community. Saint Paul reminded the Philippians (2:13): "for it is God who is at work in you." As the *Catechism of the Catholic Church* teaches, the Holy Spirit is already present in members of a religious community since the "Holy Spirit comes down and remains in the purified hearts of the baptized."[25] Luke records Saint Peter's words: "Repent and be baptized, every one of you, in the name of Jesus Christ so that your sins may be forgiven; and you will receive the gift of the Holy Spirit" (Acts 2:38). Baptism initiates an interior gift, the presence of the Holy Spirit. The charism of the consecrated life shapes and continues the experience of that baptismal presence of the Holy Spirit. John of the Cross reminds his readers that the Holy Spirit is the chief agent, principal guide, and mover of souls.[26] The Holy Spirit inspires, guides, and enlivens a religious community and its members. Nothing is more dynamic than the Holy Spirit who is Love itself, and as Saint Paul says: love "bears all things, believes all things, hopes all things, endures all things, [and] love never ends" (1 Cor 13:7–8).

The Christian tradition imagines the dynamic, loving presence of the Holy Spirit in a variety of ways, one of which perceives the Holy Spirit as a gentle breeze moving and guiding the sails of those gifted by this divine presence. Yves Congar imagines his Dominican charism this way:

Each one of us has his own gifts, his own means and his own vocation. Mine are as a Christian who prays and as a theologian who reads a great number of books and takes many notes. May I therefore be allowed to sing my

---

25 *Catechism of the Catholic Church*, 2nd ed. (Vatican City: Liberia Editrice Vaticana, 1997), no.701.

26 *The Living Flame of Love* 3.46 in *The Collected Works of St. John of the Cross*.

own song! The Spirit is breath. The wind sings in the trees. I would like, then, to be an Aeolian harp and let the breath of God make the strings vibrate and sing. Let me stretch and tune the strings—that will be the austere task of research. And then let the Spirit make them sing a clear and tuneful song of prayer and life."[27]

Eucharistic Prayer II uses a different image of the Holy Spirit's gentle but powerful activity in the following prayer of epiclesis: "Make holy, therefore, these gifts we pray by sending down your Spirit upon them like the dewfall, so that they may become for us the Body and Blood of our Lord Jesus Christ."[28] Metaphors abound in an effort to imagine the many ways in which the Holy Spirit enriches the lives of Christians and, in our context, moves religious communities to make loving decisions that include the common good. Prayer and meditation sensitize a person to the presence and promptings of the Holy Spirit, the Spirit who is Love itself. The Holy Spirit prompts those with the charism of religious life to embrace the community's mission which is, in fact, the church's mission that, in turn, is God's mission.[29] Ordinarily the Holy Spirit does not give verbal messages, but, rather, the Spirit prompts a milieu that issues in actions that are free and loving.

A charism is not a mere descriptive statement composed by a community or by an historian or a theologian, no matter

---

27   Yves Congar, *I Believe in the Spirit*, 3 vol., trans. David Smith (New York: Crossroad, 1997), I, x.

28   See John C. Nienstedt, "'Dewfall and the Prayer of Consecration," *The Catholic Spirit* (June 20, 2013), who cites William Easton for this imagery. https://thecatholicspirit.com/only-jesus/dewfall-and-the-prayer-of-consecration/, accessed May 18, 2021.

29   On mission, see Le, *Religious Life,* chapters 4–6.

how illustrious she or he may be. Carmel's charism in its deepest meaning is the gifted presence and activity of the Holy Spirit in a Carmelite community as a whole and in its members. The charism of a religious community must be clear and precise, providing reliable guidelines that remind its recipients of the presence and the stirrings of the Holy Spirit. Just as the interpretation of Scripture is incomplete until the good news is lived, so too a charism is incomplete until it is lived. Jesus taught the lawyer who asked him "who is my neighbor" by telling him the parable of the Good Samaritan and then bidding him, an expert in the law, to "Go and do likewise," that is, to live the wisdom of this parable (Lk 10:25–37). Charisms, like the Scriptures, are meant to be lived in all their fulness.

The presence of the Holy Spirit, as a personal, freely given gift, calls for gratitude, a gratitude best expressed by loving attention to the bestower of the gift. As Mary Oliver says, "Let God and the world / know you are grateful, / That the Gift has been given."[30] Since a charism is a gift of the Holy Spirit's very self, I shall comment briefly on the nature of gift.[31] A gift is a gift when it is freely given, and a gift is truly a gift when it is freely received. Reciprocity between giver and receiver is crucial. The Holy Spirit who is the Love between Father and Son freely gives his very self as gift. That gift attains completion when the Spirit is received freely, that is, when one consciously lives a Spirit-filled life. What does that Spirit-life look like when lived by the receiver? Jesus taught his followers what the presence of Love looks like with his version of Israel's great *Shema*: "you shall love the Lord

---

30   Mary Oliver, *Devotions: The Selected Poems of Mary Oliver* (New York: Penguin Press, 2017), 14.

31   On the nature of gift see Kenneth L. Schmitz, *The Gift: Creation (The Aquinas Lecture)* (Milwaukee, Wisc.: Marquette University Press, 1982). See especially 44ff.

your God with all your heart, and with all your soul, and with all
your mind, and with all your strength. [and] you shall love your
neighbor as yourself" (Mk 12:30–31).[32] Saint Paul offers a glimpse
of a Spirit-led life with his Hymn to Love: "Love is patient; love
is kind; love is not envious or boastful or arrogant or rude…It
bears all things, believes all things; hopes all things, endures all
things. Love never ends" (1 Cor 13:4–8a). In another place Paul
describes the Spirit-led life this way: "the fruit of the Spirit is love,
joy, peace, patience, kindness, generosity, faithfulness, gentleness,
and self-control" (Gal 5:22–23a). This way of love challenges
members of the Carmelite community to be all that they can be
with the help of the Holy Spirit who is God's gift to each member
of the community. The gift of self-giving Love reminds one of the
redeeming presence that inspires religious communities to do all
that they can do with God's help; God does the rest. Since the
Holy Spirit is the Carmelite charism, the title of this essay becomes
not what but Who makes a Carmelite a Carmelite?[33]

The Founder's Charism

In 1971 Saint Paul VI wrote: "Only in this way [by combining
contemplation and apostolic love] will you be able to reawaken
hearts to truth and to divine love in accordance with the charisms
of your founders who were raised up by God within His Church."
The exhortation continues: "the Council rightly insists on the
obligation of religious to be faithful to the spirit of their founders,
to their evangelical intentions and to the example of their
sanctity." Moreover, the charism of religious life "is the fruit of the
Holy Spirit who is always at work within the Church."[34] Thus did

---

32   See parallel passages: Mt 22:34–40; Lk 10:25–28.

33   John Paul II, Encyclical Letter *Dominum vivificantem On the Holy
Spirit in the Life of the Church and the World*, May 18, 1986.

34   Paul VI, Apostolic Exhortation *Evangelica testificatio: On the*

Paul VI foster within the church a conversation about the charism of founders, a conversation that continues and must continue because the human aspect of a charism must be continually renewed. Pope Francis in his Apostolic Exhortation *Evangelii gaudium* (no. 130) writes that "[a] sure sign of the authenticity of a charism is its ecclesial character, its ability to be integrated harmoniously into the life of God's holy people for the good of all," that is, for the common good. The Carmelite charism, as with all charisms, urges action on behalf of the common good.

A Carmelite scholar has reminded his readers that a charism is more complex than what appears in a brief description; his point seems to be "a warning against over-estimating the importance of a 'charism' of an order or a group."[35] On the other hand, I take it that this cautionary statement can alert communities that charisms must not be turned into facile soundbites. Brief statements about charisms need to be carefully crafted through study, prayer, and discernment so that charisms indicate what is essential to a community's spiritual identity. Carmel makes such statements to remind its members how to answer the question: Who makes a Carmelite a Carmelite? This question must be asked, not just once but often enough to keep alive the quest about what it means to follow Christ as a Carmelite.

The rule of a religious community is an abbreviation of the Gospel,[36] and so too statements about charisms are meant to be an authentic synopsis distilled from fuller elaborations. Such

Renewal of Religious Life according to the Teaching of the Second Vatican Council, June 29, 1971, no. 11. On the founder's charism, see John Carroll Futrell, "Discovering the Founder's Charism," *The Way,* Supplement 14 (Autumn 1971): 62–70.

35 Kevin Alban, "The '*Ignea Sagitta*' and the Second Council of Lyons," in *The Carmelite Rule 1207–2007*, ed. Evaldo X. Gomes et al. (Rome: Edizioni Carmelitane, 2008), 102.

36 Jean Leclercq, *La Vie Parfaite: Points de Vue sur L'Essence de L'État Religieux* (Turnhout,: Brepols, 1948), 114–21, 170.

statements are something like the prologue of John's Gospel, "a hymn that encapsulates John's view of Christ."[37] Carmel makes such brief statements to remind their young and even more seasoned members how to answer the question: Who makes a Carmelite a Carmelite? Carmel's *Rubrica prima*, that is, the initial statement of Carmelite identity that appeared in the order's medieval constitutions began with this question: "What answer is to be given to those who ask by whom and how our order began?[38] Medieval and later Carmelites knew that they must keep this question alive.[39] Blessed are those who ask questions, says the Jesuit Ladislas Orsy.[40] Carmel's charism awakens a consciousness of the abiding presence of the Holy Spirit. As followers of Jesus Christ, Carmelites are to be ever conscious of the life-giving presence of the Holy Spirit, an abiding gift that becomes ingrained in one's consciousness.

In the articulation of their charism Carmelites must avoid abstractions and jargon that reveal little of the depth and the beauty of the Carmelite tradition. Practitioners of Carmel's charism do well to engage fully in the process of discernment, a spiritual process in which a person and a community do what they can to discover God's will. Discernment requires the freedom to become the person (or community) that one is called to be and presumes rigorous historical research lest a

---

37   Raymond E. Brown, *An Introduction to the New Testament* (New York: Doubleday, 1997), 337.

38   Adrian Staring thought that this question appeared before 1247. See *Medieval Carmelite Heritage: Early Reflections on the Nature of the Order* (Rome: Institutum Carmelitanum, 1989), 12–13.

39   See the *Rubrica prima* in the medieval constitutions in *Corpus Constitutionum Ordinis Fratrum Beatissimae Virginis Mariae de Monte Carmelo*, vol. I. *Rubrica prima* (first rubric).

40   Ladislas Orsy, *Blessed Are Those Who Have Questions* (Denville, N.J.: Dimension Books, 1976).

charism be distorted without truth in one's life and ministry. Discernment has been widely explored since Vatican II,[41] and was bound to receive much more attention during the Ignatian Year, May 2021 until July 31, 2022, a year that celebrates the 500th anniversary of the conversion of Saint Ignatius of Loyola. In 1981 Ernest Larkin, O. Carm., published *Silent Presence*: *Discernment as Process and Problem,* a text that has been republished by Carmelite Media in 2021.[42]

Scripture, prayer, meditation, and theological reflection make for a lively understanding of the Carmelite tradition. Carmelite saints and blesseds as well as Carmelite authors have bequeathed a rich heritage, the fruit of their discernment. The Carmelite Formula of Life and the Carmelite Rule of 1247 conclude with a recommendation that Carmelites exercise "discretion, which is the moderator of the virtues." Discretion here is discernment. Modern authors see this recommendation from Carmel's earliest days as a reference to John Cassian's Conference 2: "On Discretion."[43] Thérèse of Lisieux, who was "really sure" that she did not possess the gift of reading souls, felt that on one occasion her words came not from her "but from Him," a discernment attained because "God was very close."[44] According to Pope Francis, discernment

---

41   Kees Waaijman, "Discernment and Biblical Spirituality: An Overview and Evaluation of Recent Research," *Acta Theologica* 33, Supplement 17 (2013): 1–12.

42   Ernest E. Larkin, *Silent Presence: Discernment as Process and Problem*, 2nd ed. (Darien, Ill.: Carmelite Media, 2021). The 2nd edition has an essay on discernment by Larkin from 2001; Ladislas Orsy, *Discernment: Theology and Practice, Communal and Personal* (Collegeville, Minn.: Liturgical Press, 2020).

43   Mullins, *St Albert*, 323; John Cassian, *The Conferences*, trans. Boniface Ramsey (New York: Paulist Press, 1997), 77–104.

44   Thérèse of Lisieux, *Story of a Soul*, 3rd ed., trans. John Clarke (Washington, D.C.: ICS Publications, 1996), 243.

"is a gift which we must implore. If we ask with confidence that the Holy Spirit grant us this gift and then develop it though prayer, reflection, reading and good counsel, then surely, we will grow in this spiritual endowment."[45] Contemplative prayer equips members of the Carmelite Family to live a discerning life, to shun superficial renderings of this precious gift, and to minister to others generously under the guidance of the Holy Spirit.[46]

Back to the Sources

One can learn much about charisms from the *Ressourcement* movement, in English "Back to the Sources." Theologians like Yves Congar, OP, and Henri de Lubac, SJ (who had a major impact on the deliberations of the Second Vatican Council) are major figures in the *Ressourcement* movement that offers a sense of the grandeur of divine gifts like charisms.[47] The poet Charles Péguy (1873–1914) saw in *Ressourcement* a movement that reveals fresh understandings and renewed energy in and through these gifts.[48] *Ressourcement* identifies important persons, events, and texts that aid in retrieving charisms and their meaning. This movement suggests that human intelligence gifted with grace can bring alive the Catholic tradition and place it into dialogue

---

45 Pope Francis, Apostolic Exhortation *Gaudete et Exultate*: *On the Call to Holiness in Today's World*," March 19, 2018, no. 166.

46 Keith J. Egan, "Contemplative Meditation: A Challenge from the Tradition," in *Handbook of Spirituality for Ministers,* vol. 2, ed. Robert J. Wicks (New York: Paulist Press, 2000), 442–55.

47 On Congar, see John W. O'Malley, *When Bishops Meet* (Cambridge, Mass. and London: Belknap Press of Harvard University Press, 2019), 124. On de Lubac, see Paul McPartlan, *Sacrament of Salvation* (Edinburgh: T&T Clark, 1995), 45–60.

48 Yves Congar, *True and False Reform in the Church*, trans. Paul Philibert (Collegeville, Minn.: Liturgical Press, 2011), 39–40n35.

with the modern world.[49] For Yves Congar, *Ressourcement* is not a "simple return to the past" rather it "asks today's questions of ancient texts but also something more and more central." It becomes "a recentering on Christ and on the paschal mystery."[50] This movement demands critical research that yields wisdom for the present and the future. For Carmelites, *Ressourcement* entails a thorough exploration of Carmel's classical texts. A classic is a person, event, or text that has an excess of meaning, an overflow of wisdom. To engage with Carmel's classics is to discover fresh understandings of Carmel's charism.[51] A partial list of these classics includes Carmel's Formula of Life, the Rule of 1247, Felip Ribot's *Institution of the First Monks*, and texts of John Soreth, Teresa of Jesus, John of the Cross, John of Saint Samson, Thérèse of Lisieux, Elizabeth of the Trinity, Titus Brandsma, and Edith Stein, to mention only the more prominent Carmelites who have penned such classical texts.

Poetry has a role in unearthing the wisdom of the Carmelite charism. Now is the time to bring on the poets, those gifted scribes who rescue us from superficiality and banality. The poet Raïssa Maritain has reflected "On Poetry as Spiritual Experience."[52] John of the Cross created stunningly beautiful poems, some of which are reports of mystical transformation. Bernard McGinn sees transformation as "the effect a divine manifestation has on transforming

---

49 Hans Boersma, *Nouvelle Théologie and Sacramental Ontology: A Return to Mystery* (Oxford: Oxford University Press, 2009). See "Ressourcement" in the index.

50 Congar, *True and False Reform*, 295.

51 David Tracy, *The Analogical Imagination* (New York: Crossroad, 1981); Stephen Okey, *A Theology of Conversation: An Introduction to David Tracy* (Collegeville, Minn.: Liturgical Press, 2018).

52 "On Poetry as Spiritual Experience," in *Raïssa's Journal*, ed. Jacques Maritain (Albany, N.Y.: Magi Books, 1974), 373–77.

the consciousness of the recipient to a deeper awareness of God's action in one's life."[53] The poet T. S. Eliot, whose sources included John of the Cross, wrote on patient waiting on God's action:

> *I said to my soul, be still, and wait without hope*
> *For hope would hope for the wrong thing; Wait without love*
> *For love would be love of the wrong thing; there is yet faith*
> *But the faith and the love and the hope are all in the waiting.*
> *Wait without thought: for you are not ready for thought:*
> *So the darkness shall be the light, and the stillness*
>   *the dancing.*[54]

For some Carmelites, poetry has risen out of their life of prayer; poets like Jessica Powers and others have the uncanny gift of expressing wisdom about the Spirit-led life in poetry.[55] Bring on the poets; they offer fresh wisdom about the Carmelite charism.[56] Without poetry much wisdom about God would be lost to humanity.

---

53   Bernard McGinn, *Mysticism in the Golden Age of Spain (1500–1650)*, vol. VI, part 2 of *The Presence of God: A History of Western Christian Mysticism* (New York: Crossroad Publishing, 2017), 13.

54   T. S. Eliot, "East Coker," *Four Quartets* in *The Complete Poems and Plays, 1909–1950* (New York: Harcourt, Brace and World, 1962), 126–27. The *Four Quartets* reveals the impact John of the Cross had on Eliot.

55   *Selected Poetry of Jessica Powers*, ed. Regina Siegfried and Robert F. Morneau (Kansas City, Mo., 1989).

56   Some poems by Carmelites: Joachim Smet, *Familiar Matter of Today* (Rome: Edizioni Carmelitane, 2007); Gervase Toelle, *Another Time, Another Place,* ed. Joachim Smet and Brennan Hill (Privately printed, no date); Toelle, *The Mantle of Elias: An Imitation* (New York: Exposition Press, 1964).

An Evolutionary Charism

A founder's charism has an afterlife, an ongoing growth, a *nachleben*, as the Germans say. A founder's charism possesses an inner wisdom that becomes more explicit in time. Since Vatican II, the emphasis by religious communities has been on the charism of their founders. John Henry Newman's *An Essay on the Development Christian Doctrine* has prompted me to explore the ongoing growth of Carmel's charism.[57] Ian Ker, an eminent scholar in matters Newman, considers this *Essay* as "certainly Newman's most famous and seminal work of theology," published but unfinished in 1845, the year that Newman became a Catholic.[58] Newman's essay had an enormous impact on Vatican II and on modern Catholic theology; this essay is a report on Newman's search and consequent conviction that Roman Catholicism is a faithful continuation of the teachings of the apostles and the fathers of the church. Newman came to this conviction as he walked with the "curious eyes of a boy" through apostolic and patristic writings. Newman's essay suggests that the teachings of the early church are like seeds that grow, unfold, and flower in the Catholic doctrine of later centuries. Newman's insight into the development of Christian doctrine suggests that a founder's charism grows, unfolds, and flowers as do seeds. When Cardinal Newman reflects on the history of doctrine, he uses the word "development." Now that there is a widespread acceptance of the notion of evolution, I prefer to speak of the evolution of a founder's charism, something like Newman's description of the unfolding of Christian doctrine. The Jesuit Roger Haight

---

57   John Henry Newman, *An Essay on the Development of Christian Doctrine*, 6th ed. (Notre Dame, Ind.: University of Notre Dame Press, 1994). This "Essay" was revised 1878.

58   Ian Ker, *The Achievement of John Henry Newman* (Notre Dame, Ind.: University of Notre Dame Press, 1990), 109.

is convinced that "[i]f our world is evolutionary, we have to incorporate its reality in our faith vision."[59] Of course, there is a difference between biological evolution and the way in which I use the concept of evolution. The latter reminds me of David Knowles's use of this concept in the title of his book *The Evolution of Medieval Thought*. He considered his book as "an endeavour to present medieval or scholastic philosophy as a direct continuation of Greek thought, coloured though it may be by its surroundings, and impoverished by many losses, but also fertilized and enriched by Christian teaching."[60] Evolution, like charism, is a divine gift lived by humans with all the vagaries of human activity, some of which can tarnish the living of a charism.

Newman's conviction that Catholicism is the same religion as that preached by the apostles became clear to him as he reviewed texts from the tradition that convinced him to forgo his Anglican commitment and to embrace Catholicism, which he did on October 9, 1845. The teachings of the Catholic Church, a faith community, developed and evolved from the apostolic era to embrace teachings at Vatican II like the surprising decree on religious freedom.[61] In this regard you may recall Newman's memorable words: "if a great idea is duly to be understood, and much more if it is to be fully exhibited...[i]t changes...in order to remain the same. In a higher world it is otherwise, but here below to live is to change, and to be perfect is to have changed often."[62] Carmel's original charism changed radically not long

---

59   Roger Haight, *Faith and Evolution: A Grace-Filled Naturalism* (Maryknoll, N.Y.: Orbis Books, 2019), 236.

60   David Knowles, *The Evolution of Medieval Thought*, 2nd ed. (London: Longman, 1988), vii.

61   Declaration on Religious Liberty *Dignitatis humanae*, December 7, 1965. In *Vatican Council II*, ed. Austin Flannery (Northport, N.Y.: Costello Publishing, Dominican Publications 1996), 551–68.

62   Newman, *An Essay on the Development of Doctrine*, 40.

after the hermits on Mount Carmel arrived in Europe where the mendicant way of life was thriving in the West. Justification for such a radical evolution required a commitment to an ongoing discernment so that Carmel's evolving charism would be faithful to its original charism.

It may seem as if historical identity and charism are separate concepts, unrelated realities in the life of a religious community. Charism primarily has to do with the graced presence of the Holy Spirit while historical research involves the application of human intelligence. On the other hand, Thomas Aquinas asserts that grace, as in the grace of a charism, respects nature, lifts nature up and perfects nature.[63] Historical research makes use of human reason while the grace of a charism raises up what reason may offer it. The baptismal grace of the Holy Spirit respects and works with human intelligence. Siblings of Thérèse of Lisieux, a doctor of the church, were distraught when they feared that their youngest sister might die during the night without the ministry of a priest. Thérèse assured her anxious siblings: "Without a doubt, it's a great grace to receive the sacraments, but, when God doesn't allow it, it's good just the same; everything is a grace."[64] With no theological training and with the near absence of formal education, Thérèse somehow knew that nature and grace are partners, that historical identity and charism work in tandem so that grace enhances and perfects nature. Thérèse had a graced instinct that affirmed that everything that is, is good, true, and beautiful, that all creation is a gift from God, including human reason. Thérèse intuited that prayer is not only a gift of grace but is also embedded in the stuff

---

63   For example: "grace does not destroy nature but perfects it." *Summa theologiae* 1.8, ad 2; cf. *Saint Thomas Aquinas:* vol. 2: *Spiritual Master*, trans. Robert Royal (Washington, D.C.: The Catholic University of America Press, 2003), 228n2.

64   *St. Thérèse of Lisieux: Last Conversations*, trans. John Clarke (Washington, D.C.: ICS Publications, 1977), 57.

of everyday life. For Thérèse of Lisieux "*prayer* is an aspiration of the heart, it is a simple glance directed to heaven, it is a cry of gratitude and love in the midst of trial as well as joy; finally, it is something great, supernatural, which expands my soul and unites me to Jesus."[65] Nature and grace are partners as are human intelligence and the self-giving presence of the Holy Spirit. The three Carmelite doctors of the church, Teresa, John, and Thérèse, as well as countless other saintly Carmelites, knew how to read the signs of the times and how to act accordingly. I have cited here and there in this essay wisdom of Carmelites who have contributed to the unfolding of Carmel's original charism. A founder's charism is not a charism's last word; rather an original charism has more to say as time goes on.

Birth of the Carmelite Charism

Prior to Vatican II, religious orders studied the history of their communities mostly in isolation from other religious communities. Since the council these communities have explored not only the history of their own communities, but they have done so in the context of other religious communities and within the ambit of religious and secular cultures not their own. What follows here is a brief review of the ingredients in Carmel's earliest or original charism as a way of applying some of what has been said of the nature of the charism of religious communities.[66] Much energy would not have been wasted had the Carmelites heeded the scholarship of the Bollandists sooner than they did.

---

65   *Story of a Soul*, 242.

66   The following Carmelite scholars consider Albert of Jerusalem as a founder of the Carmelite Order: Patrick Mullins, *St Albert of Jerusalem*, 37–38, where Mullins has citations to Vincenzo Mosca and Bruno Secondin.

But history cannot be undone; only by acceptance of the past can its wisdom be ascertained.

Christian monasticism took its rise and meaning from the good news of Jesus Christ. Early in his ministry Jesus went to Capernaum where he taught in the synagogue. His listeners "were astounded by his teaching" (Mk 1:21–22).[67] Through the centuries the good news proclaimed by Jesus awakened in women and men a call to live the way Jesus and the apostles had lived, a way known as the *vita apostolica*, the apostolic life.[68] In the fourth century and even somewhat before, Christian monasticism took root in the deserts of Egypt and Palestine. Saint Antony, often described as the "Father of Monasticism," became well known especially through Saint Athanasius's *Life of Antony*.[69] However, the beginnings of Christian monasticism—including the role of Saint Antony—are no longer so well established as was once believed. Columba Stewart, OSB, reported in 2014 that "[t]he last 50 years has seen more revisions in understanding the history of Christian monasticism than any comparable period since the Reformation." Stewart has become "all the more sensitive to the shortcomings of some of the standard monastic narratives."[70] Accordingly, I will forgo extended speculation about early monasticism. What remains true is that the Carmelite Order, like other

---

67 See also Mk 6:2, 6:51, 7:37, 10:26; Lk 4:32.

68 M-H. Vicaire, *L'Imitation des Apôtres: Moines, Chanoines et Mendiants* (Paris: Les Éditions du Cerf, 1963). English translation: *The Apostolic Life* (Chicago, Ill.: Priory Press, 1966).

69 St. Athanasius, *The Life of Saint Antony*, trans. Robert T. Meyer (New York: Newman Press, 1950) 6:51.

70 Columba Stewart, "Rethinking the History of Monasticism East and West: A Modest *tour d'horizon*," in *Prayer and Thought in Monastic Tradition: Essays in Honour of Benedicta Ward,* ed. Santha Bhattachaji, Rowan Williams, and Dominic Mattos (New York: Bloomsbury, 2014), 3–16.

medieval religious orders, had deep roots in Christianity's nascent monasticism.

When Saint Augustine (d. 430) heard about the lives of the desert Christians, especially about the life of "Antony the Egyptian," he was surprised and inspired by the flowering of monasticism, religious life or, as it is called in our time, the consecrated life.[71] The generous response of desert dwellers to Christ's "Come, follow me" has ever after captured the imagination of women and men who hunger for a deeper relationship with God. In the middle of the sixth century the Benedictine Rule opened new vistas for monasticism in the West. This rule assured women and men, in a time of widespread disorder, that the Benedictine Rule was a way to live generously the *koinonia* of the Acts of the Apostles (2:42). In time the Benedictine Rule became the major template for monasticism in the West. However, in the twelfth century monasticism began to diversify. New ways of living a religious life emerged during widespread economic, social, and intellectual upheavals that occurred in the twelfth century. Reform was in the air; new energy was evident everywhere.[72] Modern historians have discussed how best to describe the diversity of the twelfth century. Bernard McGinn says that "the notion of reform and its equivalents...is both more original and more useful as a general category for understanding twelfth-century religious culture than concepts such as renaissance."[73] The

---

71   Augustine, *Confessions*, trans. Henry Chadwick (Oxford: Oxford University Press, 1992), viii, vi, 14.

72   Giles Constable, "The Diversity of Religious Life and Acceptance of Social Pluralism in the Twelfth Century," *High Society and the Churches*, ed. Derek Beales and Geoffrey Best (Cambridge: Cambridge University Press, 1985), 29–47.

73   Bernard McGinn, *The Growth of Mysticism* (New York: Crossroad, 1994), 150. See also Bernard McGinn, "Renaissance, Humanism, and the Interpretation of the Twelfth Century," *Journal of Religion*

original Carmelite hermits entered history in an era of numerous reforms, among which was the emergence of new ways to follow Christ. The Dominican M.-D. Chenu has called this era "An Evangelical Awakening."[74] During this Gospel Awakening, Dominicans and Franciscans paved the way for the Carmelites and the Augustinian hermits to evolve from their eremitic beginnings into incipient mendicants.[75] Yet, the story of the radical transformation of Carmelite hermits into friars begs to be more fully examined.

After the First Crusade (1096–1099), westerners established the Latin Kingdom of Jerusalem, which witnessed a resurgence of monasticism including the eremitic life. As early as the eleventh century, the reformer Peter Damian, a doctor of the church, said that "it seemed as if the whole world would be turned into a hermitage."[76] However, at the Battle of Hattin on July 4, 1187, Muslim armies under the "orthodox Sunni Kurd" Saladin (1137–1193) dealt a devastating blow to the Kingdom of Jerusalem.[77] Christians living in areas under the control of Saladin were forced to seek refuge on the narrow strip of land abutting the Mediterranean Sea. Among the dislodged Latin émigrés were hermits

55, no. 4 (1975): 444–55; Giles Constable, *The Reformation of the Twelfth Century* (Cambridge: Cambridge University Press, 1996).

74   M.-D. Chenu, *Nature, Man and Society in the Twelfth Century*, ed. Jerome Taylor and Lester K. Little (Chicago and London: University of Chicago Press, 1968), 239–69.

75   See Frances Andrews, *The Other Friars: The Carmelites, Augustinian, Sack and Pied Friars in the Middle Ages* (Rochester, N.Y.: Boydell Press, 2006).

76   Peter Damian, *Vita Beati Romualdi*, ed. G. Tabacco, Fonti per la storia d'Italia 94 (Rome: Nella sede dell'Istituto, 1957), 78. Cited by Andrews, *The Other Friars*, 71.

77   Christopher Tyerman, *God's War: A New History of the Crusades* (Cambridge, Mass.: Belknap Press of Harvard University Press, 2006), 366–74.

seeking refuge along this coast where they could continue their lives of solitude.[78]

My inquiry focusses on Carmel's eremitic era which began in the final years of the twelfth century or in the early thirteenth century, certainly before August 14, 1214, when Albert of Avogadro, patriarch of Jerusalem, was assassinated by the master of the Hospital of the Holy Spirit in Acre. Albert paid a huge price for disciplining a vengeful, unstable monk. The dispersed hermits made their way to Mount Carmel after the Third Crusade had lifted the siege of Acre in July of 1191. Acre was not far from the Carmelite hermitage on Mount Carmel.

There are various opinions about who the original Carmelites were and whence they came. Joachim Smet and other scholars believe that among the dislodged hermits in the Muslim-occupied territories were hermits who found refuge on Mount Carmel, an hour's walk south of Haifa in a ravine by the *wadi 'ain es-Siāh*. The displaced hermits established a hermitage with a view looking west onto the waters of the Mediterranean Sea, waters that eventually carried Carmelite migrants to Europe.[79] Thus was born the Carmelite tradition that had its origins in the Holy Land, a sacred site from which they were too soon dispersed from the cradle of their birth. Their future lay elsewhere as they set out on a pilgrimage that has perdured through the centuries, inspiring women and men around the globe to lead lives rooted

---

78   Keith J. Egan, "The Solitude of Carmelite Prayer," in *Carmelite Prayer: A Tradition for the 21st Century*, ed. Keith J. Egan (New York: Paulist Press, 2003), 38–62.

79   Smet, *Mirror,* 5; Mullins, *St Albert,* chapter 3, see especially 79 and 108. For Mount Carmel see Carlo Cicconetti, "Luogo e Simbolo," *Dizionario Carmelitano*, ed. Emanuele Boaga and Luigi Boriello (Rome: Città Nuova, 2008), 611–16; Elias Friedman, *The Latin Hermits of Mount Carmel: A Study in Carmelite Origins* (Rome: Teresianum, 1979).

in a commitment to prayer, contemplation, and the evangelical service of others.

The hermits who settled on Mount Carmel were clearly aware that Mount Carmel was Elijah's mountain venerated by Jews, Muslims, and Christians.[80] Since Vatican II, Catholics have stressed that prophets challenge hearers to work for justice and peace. It is essential, however, to keep in mind that a prophet is one who has encountered God, and consequently, has a special message for one's community.[81] Carmelites have worked for justice and peace, but they are also called to be faithful to prayer— especially to contemplative prayer, which forms them as prophetic ministers of the Word of God. Teresa of Ávila and John the Cross describe contemplation as a transformation that is entirely God's gift.[82] Starting with Thomas Merton, modern spirituality has discovered the meaning of contemplation that includes ways of praying like Centering Prayer and Christian Meditation as taught by the Benedictine monk John Main. Ernest Larkin in his book *Contemplative Prayer for Today*: *Christian Meditation* has explored the link between Carmelite Prayer and Christian Meditation.[83]

---

80 Éliane Poirot, "The Rule as Seen from an Eastern Viewpoint: Elijah and Elisha in the Rule of Carmel," *The Carmelite Rule 1207–2007*, ed. Evaldo Xavier Gomes et al. (Rome: Edizioni Carmelitane, 2008).

81 R. N. Whybray, "Prophets/Ancient Israel," *The Oxford Companion to the Bible* (New York: Oxford University Press, 1993), 620–22.

82 For contemplation in Saints Teresa and John of the Cross, see Bernard McGinn, "Teresa of Avila Spirituality: The Contemplative in Action," 120–229, and "John of the Cross: Night, Flame, and Union," 230–335, in McGinn, *Mysticism in the Golden Age of Spain (1500–1650)*; see also "contemplation" in the index.

83 See Ernest Larkin, *Contemplative Prayer for Today*: *Christian Meditation* (Singapore: Medio Media, 2007). See also Keith J. Egan, "Contemplative Meditation: A Challenge from the Tradition," *Handbook of Spirituality for Ministers*, vol. 2, 442–55; Thomas Merton, *New Seeds of Contemplation* (New York: New Directions, 1972).

The Formula of Life

Sometime between 1206 and 1214,[84] the hermits on Mount Carmel asked Albert, patriarch of Jerusalem, to compose for them a document describing how they should live.[85] Albert's response is known as their "Formula of Life."[86] This Formula is a letter, the original of which is no longer extant. It is rich in biblical citations and allusions and describes a very simple life of solitude and prayer.[87] When Albert arrived in the Holy Land, he was unable to reside in Jerusalem because it was in the hands of Muslims, so he established his residence in Acre, a port city north of Haifa about eighteen miles from the Carmelite hermitage. The Formula of Life is addressed to "B. and the other hermits...who reside near the spring on Mount Carmel."[88] The Formula of Life, Carmel's

---

84 Innocent III appointed Albert Avogadro patriarch of Jerusalem in 1205. Albert arrived in Acre in 1206. In 1214 Albert was assassinated by a disgruntled monk of the Hospital of the Holy Spirit during a procession that occurred on September 14, the Feast of the Exaltation of the Cross.

85 Mullins, *St Albert,* chapter 4.

86 For editions of the Formula of Life, see Joachim Smet, *Latin Religious Houses*, 90n80.

    Saint Teresa did not know the Formula of Life. She referred to the rule approved by Innocent IV in 1247 as the order's *regla primera* or *primitiva*. Otger Steggink, *La Reforma del Carmelo Español* (Rome: Institutum Carmelitanum, 1965), index and 506 for citations to what Teresa called the *regla primera o primitiva*. The 2nd edition of this work has not been available to the author.

87 See James McCaffrey, *The Carmelite Charism: Exploring the Biblical Roots* (Dublin: Veritas, 2004), chapter 3: "The Carmelite Rule: A Gospel Approach."

88 In 1507 the initial "B." was expanded to Brocard. Joachim Smet commented: "in the opinion of the late Adrian Staring, specialist in medieval Carmelite history, there is no reason to suspect this solution." Joachim Smet, "The Carmelite Rule after 750 Years," *Carmelus* 44 (1997): 37n88.

oldest document, has pride of place among all Carmelite sources. With a few changes, the Formula became a rule approved by Pope Innocent IV on October 1, 1247,[89] a truly a memorable day which initiated the transformation of the hermits from Mount Carmel into an order of friars.

In this essay I concentrate on the Formula of Life, because it describes the eremitic life of Carmelites, before Innocent IV approved the modified Formula that became an ecclesial rule making possible the entry of the Carmelite order into the ranks of the mendicants. I see the era between the settlement on Mount Carmel and 1247 to be the era of Carmel's original or founders' charism, which contains the seeds that evolved into mendicancy. My hope is to follow this essay with an exploration of the transformation of Carmelite hermits into friars. Here I will concentrate on the Formula of Life that has the ingredients of Carmel's original charism. When I speak of this charism here, I refer to its ingredients because the charism of a religious community becomes an ecclesial charism when members of the community receive regional ecclesiastical approval or papal approval of their charism.

The Formula of Life describes how the Carmelite hermits are to live "in allegiance to Jesus Christ," who was and is *the* focus of their existence.[90] The hermitage on Mount Carmel reminds one of a small Palestinian *laura*.[91] Each hermit has a small cell (Latin:

---

89 Patrick Mullins, "The Carmelite Rule: Text and Authors," in *Celebrating St. Albert and his Rule: Rules, Devotion, Orthodoxy and Dissent*, ed. Michelle M. Sauer and Kevin J. Alban (Rome: Edizioni Carmelitane, 2017), 25–34.

90 Mullins, *St Albert*, 40, 147, 153, translates "in obsequio Iesu Christi" as "vassals of Jesus Christ." I favor the translation by Bede Edwards in *The Rule of Saint Albert* (Aylesford and Kensington, UK: Carmelite Press, 1973), 78–79: "allegiance to Jesus Christ."

91 William Harmless, *Desert Christians: An Introduction to the Literature of Early Monasticism* (Oxford University Press, 2004), 433–34.

celulla) separated from the others.[92] The hermits prayed the psalms on their own, and they ate their meals alone. In the early morning the hermits gathered for daily Mass in the oratory located in the center of the surrounding cells. There the hermits celebrated Eucharist "when it can be done conveniently."[93] Besides the celebration of Mass, the only other time that the hermits gathered as a community was on Sundays when they conversed about their spiritual lives, a time set aside for communal discernment and fraternal correction.[94] The hermits fasted from the feast of the Exaltation of the Cross on September 14th until Easter Sunday. They abstained from meat except when illness, debility, or another reason allowed meat. The hermits engaged in manual labor. They were to remain in their small cells or nearby meditating day and night on the Law of the Lord (Ps 1:2). Silence, solitude, prayer, and contemplation were the preoccupation of Carmel's hermits whose lives were marked by utter simplicity. The Dutch Carmelite Kees Waaijman calls the place where this Formula of Life was lived a "mystical space,"[95] a space where spiritual transformation can occur. One can only try to imagine what took place in the minds and hearts of Carmel's hermits as they lived, prayed, and labored in a place designed to free them from the obstacles to love of Christ and of their brother hermits.

92 Writing toward the end of the thirteenth century, an Augustinian canon of Barnwell Priory found it memorable that each Carmelite at Chesterton near Cambridge had his own cell. Keith J. Egan, "The Carmelites Turn to Cambridge," *The Land of Carmel: Essays in Honor of Joachim Smet, O. Carm.*, ed. Paul Chandler and Keith J. Egan (Rome: Institutum Carmelitanum), 160.

93 The words "when it can be done conveniently" may have anticipated times when no priest would be present in the community.

94 See Mullins, *St Albert*, "Formula of Life and the Rule of 1247," chapter 15.

95 Kees Waaijman, *The Mystical Space of Carmel: A Commentary on the Rule*, trans. John Vriend (Louvain: Peeters, 1999), title and 3.

The Formula of Life has no mention of an external ministry by the hermits, nor does it speak of Elijah and Mary, who became and remain major figures in the Carmelite Tradition. While Elijah is not mentioned in the Formula of Life nor in the Rule, these hermits on Mount Carmel were keenly aware that they lived on a site sacred to the memory of the Elijah who encountered God in the "sound of sheer silence" (1 Kgs 19:12).[96] Concerning the genesis of Marian devotion to the Blessed Virgin, a French pilgrim, about the year 1220, made this notation: "On the slope of this same mountain is a very fair place and delicious where there is a little church of our Lady."[97] The dedication of the hermits' oratory to the Blessed Virgin is the earliest mention of Mary in the Carmelite tradition. This devotion to the Virgin has grown and perdured over the centuries in Carmelite life, liturgy, and literature. One illustration of this relationship is the title in its various forms that the Carmelites adopted: Brothers of the Most Blessed Virgin Mary of Mount Carmel.[98]

The Formula of Life envisions only the hermitage on Mount Carmel with no intimation of what lay ahead for Mount Carmel's hermits who began to leave the Holy Land about 1238 to make foundations in Europe.[99] Beside the hermitage on Mount Carmel the Carmelites established in Palestine two other foundations: Acre sometime after 1247 and Tyre before August 5, 1262. These two foundations were made after the papal approval of

---

96 Craig Morrison, "Handing on the Mantle: The Transmission of the Elijah Cycle in the Biblical Versions," in *Master of the Sacred Page: Essays and Articles in Honor of Roland E. Murphy, O. Carm.*, ed. Keith J. Egan and Craig E. Morrison (Washington, D.C.: The Carmelite Institute, 1997), 109–29.

97 Mullins, *St Albert*, 17.

98 On the Marian title of the order see Emanuele Boaga, *The Lady of the Place: Mary in the History and in the Life of Carmel* (Rome: Edizioni Carmelitane, 2001), 24–25.

99 Smet, *Mirror of Carmel*, 9.

the Rule.[100] These two foundations and the hermitage on Mount Carmel ceased to exist before or in 1291. Joachim Smet vividly captured, in a poem composed in 1938, the forced departure of Carmelites with a special devotion to Mary from the Holy Land. The Carmelites, like other orders, honored Mary by singing in the evening the Salve Regina hymn. Smet imagined some forbearers being martyred before they could leave the Holy Land for Europe, where the Dominicans and the Franciscans had sketched a new way of serving their neighbors in word and sacrament.

The Salve Regina Hour

Mount Carmel's sides are tall and steep
And bright with many a flower,
But not too steep for the Turk to climb
At the Salve Regina Hour.

The sun sank down in the Western sea,
Sank down in his blood-red bower,
But not so red as the choir stalls
At the Salve Regina Hour.

"We heard the tinkling of swords and spear
Like the Vesper-bell's brittle shower,
And the breathing of horses that rode from dawn
To the Salve Regina hour.

"Some Christian knights are come," we said,
"To mingle their voices with ours,

---

100 Joachim Smet, "The Latin Religious Houses in Crusader Palestine, An Inventory," 89–92. This essay can be accessed at https:/zenodo.org/record/3960485. Information kindly provided by Paul Chandler, O. Carm.

To pray for the weal of the Savior's tomb
At the Salve Regina hour."

But the Turks rushed in with their simitars
In a flashing tide of power,
And butchered the hermits as they sang
At the Salve Regina Hour.

"We pray you, brethren, to think of us
Whom sword has sought to devour,
To finish the song that we once began
At the Salve Regina Hour."[101]

Earlier in the thirteenth century the hermits on Mount Carmel caught the eye of a discerning observer of religious communities. Jacques de Vitry, bishop of Acre (1216–1228) and later a cardinal, praised Carmel's hermits with this entry: "Others, in imitation of the holy anchorite the prophet Elijah, led solitary lives on Mount Carmel...near the well called Elijah's well, not far from the convent of St. Margaret the Virgin, where in little comb-like cells, those bees of the Lord laid up sweet spiritual honey."[102]

101 Smet, "The Salve Regina Hour," in Smet, *Familiar Matter of Today,* 85. For the legendary massacre of the Carmelite hermits in 1291, see Felip Ribot, *The Ten Books on the Way of Life and the Great Deeds of the Carmelites,* ed. and trans. Richard Copsey (Faversham, Kent, UK and Rome: Saint Albert's Press and Edizioni Carmelitane, 2005), xii–xiii.

102 Smet, *Mirror of Carmel,* 3. There are some further items to be considered in exploring the identity and the charism of Carmel before 1247: the impact of choosing to live and pray in the Holy Land, the foundations made in England (Hulne, Aylesford, Bradmer/ Burnham Norton, and Losenham) also in Cyprus, Sicily and Southern France. For the English foundations see Keith J. Egan,

Such was the birth of the original Carmelite charism, a work of the Holy Spirit, who inspired men to live their love of God in solitude, a solitude made possible by the vigilance of a prior whose cell was at the entrance to the hermitage and by the love of their fellow hermits. Saint Albert's Formula of Life describes an eremitic community with deep roots in Palestinian monasticism. These hermits on Mount Carmel made a commitment: to follow and to imitate Jesus Christ in a fraternal community that lived simply, performed manual labor, cherished solitude, prayer, contemplation, and celebrated the Eucharist each day when it was possible to do so.[103]

Having pondered in this essay and for some long time the Formula of Life as well as the few footprints that Carmel's hermits left behind them, I suggest that the Founders' Charism of the Carmelite Order consists in the first hermits unknown by name and Saint Albert of Jerusalem who composed the Formula of Life at their request.

Conclusion

For a long time, I have been interested in Carmelite identity and the meaning of the Carmelite charism. When I was invited in 2020 to deliver the First Annual Lecture in Carmelite Studies at The Catholic University of America, I was delighted to do so

---

"Medieval Carmelite Houses, England and Wales," *Carmelus* 16 (1969): 142–226.

103 For an example of two modern renditions of the Carmelite charism of the Friars, see, for the O.Carms., the 1995 Constitutions of the Carmelites of the Ancient Observance (https:www.carmelite.org/sites/default/files/carmeliteconstitutions1995.pdf); and for the Discalced, "Being Discalced Carmelite Friars Today: Declaration on the Carmelite-Teresian Charism," approved by the 2021 General Chapter of the Discalced Carmelites (https://www.carmelitaniscalzi.com/en/documents/general-chapters/declaration-on-the-carmelite-teresian-charism/).

even though the lecture had to be delivered virtually in February of 2021. To prepare this lecture for publication, I wanted to clarify for myself and others the meaning of charism as it has evolved since the Second Vatican Council and to initiate conversations about the Carmelite charism. Such conversations can lead to the formation of a Carmelite imagination that enlivens the Carmelite Tradition.

There are a few takeaways from this essay that I will mention briefly. First, the study of the Carmelite Tradition demands a firm commitment to rigorous scholarship that instills confidence in the Carmelite charism. Furthermore, formators need to introduce younger members of the Carmelite Family to reliable histories of the order. While a charism is a supernatural gift, it is meant to be lived in the everyday circumstances of life and ministry.

The most consequential aspect of the Carmelite charism is that this charism is a freely given divine gift, a personal self-giving of the Holy Spirit. This gift, which is appropriated to the Holy Spirit, includes the presence of the Father and the Son, and calls for a free, personal response of loving attention to the God who is love, a gift that urges Carmelites to act habitually for the common good.

I conclude this essay with a word from two of the three Carmelite doctors of the church, Teresa of Jesus and John of the Cross. Neither Teresa of Jesus nor John of the Cross used the word charism (*carisma*). However, Teresa had in mind Mount Carmel's nameless hermits when she wrote: "So I say now that all of us who wear the habit of Carmel are called to prayer and contemplation. This call explains our origin; we are the descendants of men who felt this call, of those holy Fathers on Mount Carmel who in such solitude and contempt for the world sought this treasure, this precious pearl of contemplation."[104]

---

104 *The Interior Castle*, 5.1.2 in *The Collected Works of St. Teresa of Avila*.

An abiding consciousness of the presence of the Holy Spirit created in John of the Cross a heart filled with gratitude. With the simplicity born of humility, Brother John of the Cross burst into lyrical gratitude when he became aware of the many gifts that the Holy Spirit bestowed on his sisters and brothers in Carmel. One of John's "Sayings of Light and Love" (no. 27) is filled with gratitude and joy that almost overwhelms him when he recalls these gifts:

> Mine are the heavens and mine is the earth. Mine are the nations, the just are mine, and mine the sinners. The angels are mine, and the Mother of God, and all things are mine; and God himself is mine and for me, because Christ is mine and all for me. What do you ask, then, and seek, my soul? Yours is all of this, and all is for you. Do not engage yourself in something less or pay heed to the crumbs that fall from your Father's table. Go forth and exult in your Glory! Hide yourself in it and rejoice, and you will obtain the supplications of your heart.[105]

Keith J. Egan, T. O. Carm.
Saint Mary's College and the University of Notre Dame

---

105 "The Sayings of Light and Love" in *The Collected Works of St. John of the Cross* (1991), 87–88.

Bibliography

Ackerman, Jane. *Elijah, Prophet of Carmel*. Washington, D.C.:
     ICS Publications, 2003.
Alban, Kevin. "The '*Ignea Sagitta*' and the Second Council of Lyons."
     In *The Carmelite Rule 1207–2007*. Edited by Evaldo X.
     Gomes et al. Rome: Edizioni Carmelitane, 2008.
Alford, Elisée. *Les missions des Carmes Déchaux, 1575–1975*.
     Présence du Carmel 13. Paris: Desclée de Brouwer, 1977.
Ana de San Bartolomé. *Autobiography and Other Writings*. Trans-
     lated by Darcy Donohue. The Other Voice in Early
     Modern Europe Series. Chicago: University of Chicago
     Press, 2008.
Andrews, Frances. *The Other Friars: The Carmelites, Augustinian,
     Sack and Pied Friars in the Middle Ages*. Rochester, N.Y.:
     Boydell Press, 2006.
Arenal, Electa, and Stacey Schlau. *Untold Sisters: Hispanic Nuns
     in Their Own Works*. Albuquerque, N.Mex.: University
     of New Mexico Press, 1989.
Athanasius, St. *The Life of Saint Antony*. Translated by Robert T.
     Meyer. New York: Newman Press, 1950.
Augustine. *Confessions*. Translated by Henry Chadwick. Oxford:
     Oxford University Press, 1992.
Beauregard, Mario. "Neural Correlates of a Mystical Experience
     in Carmelite Nuns." *Neuroscience Letters* 405 (September
     25, 2006): 186–90.

Bergström-Allen, Johan, ed. *Climbing the Mountain*: *The Carmelite Journey*. Faversham, Kent, UK: Saint Albert's Press, 2010.

Boaga, Emanuele. *The Lady of the Place: Mary in the History and in the Life of Carmel*. Rome: Edizioni Carmelitane, 2001.

Boersma, Hans. *Nouvelle Théologie and Sacramental Ontology: A Return to Mystery*. Oxford: Oxford University Press, 2009.

Bolland, Joannis, Godefridus Henschenius, Jean Baptiste Carnandet. *Acta Sanctorum*. Paris: Victorem Palmé, 1863. Available online at the Digital Library, Villanova University, Philadelphia, Pa. https://digital.library.villanova.edu/Item/vudl:621722#?c=&m=&s=&cv=&xywh=-703%2C-38%2C1862%2C743.

Brandsma, Titus. *Carmelite Mysticism: Historical Sketches*. Chicago: Carmelite Press, 1936.

Brown, Raymond E. *An Introduction to the New Testament*. New York: Doubleday, 1997.

Cassian, John. *The Conferences*. Translated by Boniface Ramsey. New York: Paulist Press, 1997.

Cassidy, Laurie, and M. Shawn Copeland, eds. *Desire, Darkness, and Hope: Theology in a Time of Impasse: Engaging the Thought of Constance FitzGerald. OCD*. Collegeville, Minn.: Liturgical Press, 2021.

Catechism of the Catholic Church, 2nd ed. Vatican City: Liberia Editrice Vaticana, 1997.

Cecilia de Nacimiento. *Obras Completas*. Edited by José M. Diaz Ceron. Madrid: Editorial de Espiritualidad, 1971.

———. *Journeys of a Mystical Soul in Poetry and Prose*. Edited by Kevin Donnelly and Sandra Sider. Toronto: Centre for Reformation and Renaissance Studies, 2012.

Chaucer, Geoffrey. *The Canterbury Tales*. Translated by Nevill Coghill. London: Penguin Books, 1977.

Chenu, M.-D. *Nature, Man and Society in the Twelfth Century.* Edited by Jerome Taylor and Lester K. Little. Chicago and London: University of Chicago Press, 1968.

Cicconetti, Carlo. "Luogo e Simbolo." In *Dizionario Carmelitano*, edited by Emanuele Boaga and Luigi Boriello, 20: 611–16. Rome: Città Nuova, 2008.

Clarke, Hugh, and Bede Edwards, eds. *The Rule of Saint Albert.* Aylesford and Kensington, UK: Carmelite Press, 1973.

Code of Canon Law. Vatican City: Libreria Editrice Vaticana, 1983.

Congar, Yves. *I Believe in the Spirit*, 3 vol. Translated by David Smith. New York: Crossroad, 1997.

———. *True and False Reform in the Church.* Translated by Paul Philibert. Collegeville, Minn.: Liturgical Press, 2011.

Constable, Giles. "The Diversity of Religious Life and Acceptance of Social Pluralism in the Twelfth Century." In *High Society and the Churches*, edited by Derek Beales and Geoffrey Best, 29–47. Cambridge: Cambridge University Press, 1985.

Copsey, Richard. "Establishment, Identity and Papal Approval: The Carmelite Order's Creation of Its Legendary History." *Carmelus* 47 (2000): 41–53.

Corpus Constitutionum Ordinis Fratrum Beatissimae Virginis Mariae de Monte Carmelo. 4 vols. Edited by Edison Tinambunan and Emanuele Boaga. Rome: Edizioni Carmelitane, 2011.

Constable, Giles. "The Ideal of the Imitation of Christ." In *Three Studies in Medieval Religious and Social Thought.* Cambridge: Cambridge University Press, 1995.

———. *The Reformation of the Twelfth Century.* Cambridge: Cambridge University Press, 1996.

Damian, Peter. *Vita Beati Romualdi.* Edited by G. Tabacco. Fonti per la storia d'Italia 94. Rome: Nella sede dell'Istituto, 1957.

Efrén de la Madre de Dios and Otger Steggink, s.v., "Carmelite Spiri-
        tuality." In *New Catholic Encyclopedia,* edited by William J.
        McDonald, et al. New York: McGraw-Hill, 1967.

Egan, Keith J. "The Establishment and Early Development of the
        Carmelite Order in England." Unpublished Doctoral
        Dissertation. University of Cambridge, 1965.

——. "Medieval Carmelite Houses, England and Wales."
        Carmelus 16 (1969): 142–226.

——. "Dom David Knowles, 1896–1974." *The Benedictine
        Review* 27, no. 3 (1976): 235–46.

——. "Dom David Knowles." *The New Catholic Encyclopedia*,
        2nd ed., vol. 17. 1978.

——. "The Carmelites Turn to Cambridge." In *The Land of
        Carmel: Essays in Honor of Joachim Smet, O. Carm,*
        edited by Paul Chandler and Keith J. Egan, 155–170.
        Rome: Institutum Carmelitanum, 1991.

——. "Contemplative Meditation: A Challenge from the
        Tradition." In *Handbook of Spirituality for Ministers*. Vol.
        2, edited by Robert J. Wicks. New York: Paulist Press, 2000.

——. "The Solitude of Carmelite Prayer." In *Carmelite Prayer:
        A Tradition for the 21st Century*, edited by Keith J. Egan,
        38–62. New York: Paulist Press, 2003.

——. "Obituary: Joachim F. Smet, O. Carm. (1915–2011)." *The
        Catholic Historical Review* 98, no. 1 (2012): 196–98.

——. *What Makes a Carmelite a Carmelite*? Washington D.C.:
        The Catholic University Press, 2022.

Eliot, T. S. "East Coker." No. 2 of *Four Quartets*. In *The Complete
        Poems and Plays*, 1909–1950. New York: Harcourt,
        Brace and World, 1962.

Emery, Richard W. "The Second Council of Lyons and the
        Mendicant Orders." *The Catholic Historical Review* 39,
        no. 3 (October 1953): 257–71.

Episcopal Church. *A Great Cloud of Witnesses: A Calendar of Commemorations*. New York: Church Publishing, 2016.

Erikson, Erik. *Childhood and Society*, 2nd ed. New York: W. W. Norton, 1963.

———. *Identity: Youth and Crisis*. New York: W.W. Norton, 1968.

Farrell, Brian. "Spiritual Ecumenism: The Inescapable Way Forward." *People on the Move* 97 Supplement (April 2005).

Farrelly, M. John. "Holy Spirit." In *The New Dictionary of Catholic Spirituality*, edited by Michael Downey, 492–503. Collegeville, Minn.: Liturgical Press, 1993.

Fastiggi, Robert L. "Charism." *New Catholic Encyclopedia*. 2nd.ed. *Supplement*, vol. 3, edited by Fastiggi, 254–58. Detroit: Gale, 2010.

FitzGerald, Constance. "From Impasse to Prophetic Hope: Crisis of Memory." *Proceedings of the Catholic Theological Society of America* 64 (2009): 21–42.

Florencio del Niño Jesús. *La Orden de Santa Teresa, la Fundación de la Propaganda Fidei, y las Misiones Carmelitanas*. Madrid: Nieto y Compañía, 1923.

———. "Impasse and Dark Night." In *Living with Apocalypse: Spiritual Resources for Social Compassion*. Edited by Tilden Edwards. San Francisco: Harper & Row, 1984.

Foley, G. "Charisms in Religious Life." In *New Catholic Encyclopedia*. 2nd ed., vol. 3, 393–94. Detroit: Gale, 2003.

Francis. *Gaudete et Exultate: On the Call to Holiness in Today's World*. Apostolic Exhortation. March 19, 2018.

Friedman, Elias. *The Latin Hermits of Mount Carmel: A Study in Carmelite Origins*. Rome: Teresianum, 1979.

Futrell, John Carroll. "Discovering the Founder's Charism." *The Way*. Supplement 14 (Autumn 1971): 62–70.

Haight, Roger. *Faith and Evolution: A Grace-Filled Naturalism*. Maryknoll, N.Y.: Orbis Books, 2019.

Harmless, William. *Desert Christians: An Introduction to the Literature of Early Monasticism*. Oxford: Oxford University Press, 2004.

Healy, Kilian. *Prophet of Fire*. Rome: Edizioni Carmelitane, 1990.

Howe, Elizabeth Teresa. *The Visionary Life of Madre Ana de San Agustín*. Woodbridge, Suffolk: Tamesis, 2004.

John of the Cross. *The Collected Works of St. John of the Cross,*. Edited and translated by Kieran Kavanaugh and Otilio Rodriguez. Washington, D.C.: ICS Publications, 1991.

John Paul II. "Master in the Faith: Apostolic Letter for the Fourth Centenary of the Death of Saint John of the Cross." *L'Osservatore Romano* 52, no. 14. English edition. December 24, 1990.

———. *Dominum vivificantem On the Holy Spirit in the Life of the Church and the World*. Encyclical Letter. May 18, 1986.

———. "Message for the 550th Anniversary of the Papal Bull, *Cum nulla*, to Joseph Chalmers, O. Carm., Prior General of the Carmelite Order." Vatican City, October 7, 2002.

John XXIII. *Humanae salutis*. Apostolic Constitution. December 25, 1961. In *Acta Apostolicae Sedis* 54 (1962).

Joseph of the Holy Spirit. *Cursus Theologiae Mystico-Scholasticae,* 6 vols. Bruges, Belgium: Carolum Beyaert, 1925.

Ker, Ian. *The Achievement of John Henry Newman*. Notre Dame, Ind.: University of Notre Dame Press, 1990.

Knowles, David. "The Bollandists." In *Great Historical Enterprises*: *History and Problems in Monastic History*. London: Thomas Nelson and Sons, 1963.

———. *The Evolution of Medieval Thought*. 2nd ed. London: Longman, 1988.

Larkin, Ernest E. *Contemplative Prayer for Today*: *Christian Meditation*. Singapore: Medio Media, 2007.

———. *Silent Presence: Discernment as Process and Problem*. 2nd ed. Darien, Ill.: Carmelite Media, 2021.

Laurent, M.-H. "La Lettre 'Quae honorem conditoris,' (October 1,1247)." *Ephemerides Carmeliticae* 2 (1948): 5–16.

Leclercq, Jean. *La Vie Parfaite: Points de Vue sur L'Essence de L'État Religieux.* Turnhout: Brepols, 1948.

——. "Lérémitismo en Occident 'jusqu á l'an mil." In *L'Eremitismo en occidente nei secoli XI e XII. Atti della Seconda Settimana Internationale di Studio, Mendola.* AA.VV, 27–44. Milan: Società editrice Vita et Pensierno, 1965.

Maritain, Raïssa. "On Poetry as Spiritual Experience." In *Raïssa's Journal,* edited by Jacques Maritain, 303–8. Albany, N.Y.: Magi Books, 1974.

María de San José Salazar. *Book for the Hour of Recreation.* Translated by Alison Weber. Chicago: University of Chicago Press, 2002.

Matthew, Iain. "Visualising Christology: Llama de amor viva and the Resurrection." *Teresianum* 68, no. 1 (2017): 87–125.

McCaffrey, James. *The Carmelite Charism: Exploring the Biblical Roots.* Dublin: Veritas, 2004.

McGinn, Bernard. "Renaissance, Humanism, and the Interpretation of the Twelfth Century." *Journal of Religion* 55, no. 4 (1975): 444–55.

——. *The Growth of Mysticism.* New York: Crossroad, 1994.

——. "The Role of the Carmelites in the History of Western Mysticism." In *Carmel and Contemplation: Transforming Human Consciousness.* Edited by Kevin Culligan and Regis Jordan. *Carmelite Studies* 8. Washington, D.C.: ICS Publications, 2000.

——. *Mysticism in the Golden Age of Spain (1500–1650).* Vol. 1, part 2 of *The Presence of God: A History of Western Mysticism.* New York: Herder & Herder, 2017.

McIntosh, Mark. *Mystical Theology: The Integrity of Spirituality and Theology.* Malden, Mass.: Blackwell Publishers, 1998.

McPartlan, Paul. *Sacrament of Salvation*. Edinburgh: T&T Clark, 1995.

Merton, Thomas. *New Seeds of Contemplation*. New York: New Directions, 1972.

Metz, Johann Baptist. *Faith in History and Society: Toward a Practical Fundamental Theology*. Translated by David Smith. New York: Crossroad Book, Seabury Press, 1980.

Mullins, Patrick. *St Albert of Jerusalem and the Roots of Carmelite Spirituality*. Rome: Edizioni Carmelitane, 2012.

———. "The Carmelite Rule: Text and Authors." In *Celebrating St. Albert and His Rule*: *Rules, Devotion, Orthodoxy and Dissent*. Edited by Michelle M. Sauer and Kevin J. Alban. Rome: Edizioni Carmelitane, 2017.

Murphy, Roland E. "Elijah the Prophet." In *Experiencing Our Biblical Heritage*. Peabody, Mass.: Hendrickson Publishers, 2001.

Newman, John Henry. *An Essay on the Development of Christian Doctrine*, 6th ed. Notre Dame, Ind.: University of Notre Dame Press, 1994.

O'Donnell, Christopher. "Maria nel Carmelo." In *Dizionario Carmelitano*, edited by Emanuele Boaga and Luigi Borriello, 539–46. Rome: Città Nuova, 2008.

O'Malley, John W. *When Bishops Meet*. Cambridge, Mass.: Belknap Press of Harvard University Press, 2019.

Oliver, Mary. *Devotions: The Selected Poems of Mary Oliver*. New York: Penguin Press, 2017.

Okey, Stephen. *A Theology of Conversation*: *An Introduction to David Tracy*. Collegeville, Minn.: Liturgical Press, 2018.

Orsy, Ladislas. *Blessed Are Those Who Have Questions*. Denville, N.J.: Dimension Books, 1976.

———. *Discernment: Theology and Practice, Communal and Personal*. Collegeville, Minn.: Liturgical Press, 2020.

Paul VI. *Evangelica testificatio: On the Renewal of Religious Life according to the Teaching of the Second Vatican Council*. Apostolic Exhortation. June 29, 1971.

Payne, Steven. *The Carmelite Tradition*. Collegeville, Minn.: Liturgical Press, 2011.

Poirot, Éliane. "The Rule as Seen from an Eastern Viewpoint: Elijah and Elisha in the Rule of Carmel." *The Carmelite Rule 1207–2007*. Edited by Evaldo Xavier Gomes et al. Rome: Edizioni Carmelitane, 2008.

Ribot, Felip. *The Ten Books on the Way of Life and the Great Deeds of the Carmelites*. Edited and translated by Richard Copsey. Faversham, Kent, UK: Saint Albert's Press, 2005.

Roefs, Victor J. G. "The Earliest Evidence Concerning the Carmelite Order." Translated by Sean O'Leary. *The Sword* 19 (1956): 224–45.

Röhrkasten, Jens and Coralie Zermatten, eds. *Historiography and Identity: Responses to Medieval Carmelite Culture*. Vienna: LIT Verlag, 2017.

Rohrbach, Peter-Thomas. *Journey to Carith*. New York: Doubleday & Co., 1966.

Root, Michael. "Ecumenical Winter." *First Things* 286 (October 2018).

Saggi, Ludovico, ed. *Santi del Carmelo*. Rome: Institutum Carmelitanum, 1972.

Schmitz, Kenneth L. *The Gift: Creation (The Aquinas Lecture)*. Milwaukee, Wisc.: Marquette University Press, 1982.

Schneiders, Sandra M. "Foreword." to*Religious Life: A Reflective Examination of Its Charism and Mission for Today* by Loan Le. Newcastle upon Tyne: Cambridge Scholars, 2016.

Siegfried, Regina, and Robert F. Morneau. *Selected Poetry of Jessica Powers*. Kansas City, Mo., 1989.

Smet, Joachim. *The Carmelites: A History of the Brothers of Our Lady of Mount Carmel*. Vol.1. rev. ed. Darien, Ill.: Carmelite Spiritual Center, 1988.

———. "The Carmelite Rule after 750 Years." *Carmelus* 44 (1997): 21–47.

———. *Familiar Matter of Today*. Rome: Edizioni Carmelitane, 2007.

———. *The Mirror of Carmel*. Darien, Ill.: Carmelite Media, 2011.

———. "The Latin Religious Houses in Crusader Palestine: An Inventory." Unpublished, posted July 26, 2020. https:/ zenodo.org/record/3960485

Špidlík, Tomáš. *The Spirituality of the Christian East: A Systematic Handbook*. Translated by Anthony P. Gythiel. Kalamazoo, Mich.: Cistercian Publications, 1986.

Staring, Adrianus, ed. *Medieval Carmelite Heritage: Early Reflections on the Nature of the Order*. Rome: Institutum Carmelitanum, 1989.

Stein, Edith. "On the History and Spirit of Carmel." In *The Hidden Life: Hagiographic Essays, Meditations, Spiritual Texts*. Translated by Waltraut Stein. Edited by Lucy Gelber and Michael Linssen. Washington, D.C.: ICS Publications, 1992.

Stewart, Columba. "Rethinking the History of Monasticism East and West: A Modest *tour d'horizon*." In *Prayer and Thought in Monastic Tradition: Essays in Honour of Benedicta Ward*, edited by Santha Bhattachaji, Rowan Williams, and Dominic Mattos, 3–16. New York: Bloomsbury, 2014.

Tanner, Norman P. *Decrees of the Ecumenical Councils*. Washington, D.C.: Georgetown University Press, 1990.

Teresa of Ávila. *The Collected Works of St. Teresa of Ávila*. 3 vols. Translated by Kieran Kavanaugh and Otilio Rodriguez. Washington, D.C.: ICS Publications, 1976–1986.

Thérèse of Lisieux. *Story of a Soul*. 3rd ed., translated by John Clarke. Washington, D.C.: ICS Publications, 1996.

———. *St. Thérèse of Lisieux: Last Conversations*. Translated by John Clarke. Washington, D.C.: ICS Publications, 1977.

Thompson, William. *Fire and Light: The Saints and Theology: On Consulting the Saints, Mystics, and Martyrs in Theology*. Mahwah, N.J.: Paulist Press, 1987.

Toelle, Gervase. *The Mantle of Elias: An Imitation*. New York: Exposition Press, 1964.

———. *Another Time, Another Place,* ed. Joachim Smet and Brennan Hill. Lakes Region Lithography Co, 1972.

Torrell, Jean-Pierre. *Saint Thomas Aquinas:* vol. 2: *Spiritual Master*. Translated by Robert Royal. Washington, D.C.: The Catholic University of America Press, 2003.

Tracy, David. *The Analogical Imagination*. New York: Crossroad, 1981.

Tyerman, Christopher. *God's War: A New History of the Crusades*. Cambridge, Mass.: Belknap Press of Harvard University Press, 2006.

Urkiza, Julián, ed., *Obras Completas de la Beata Ana de San Bartolomé*. 2 vols. Rome: Edizioni Teresianum, 1985.

Vatican Council II. *Constitutions, Decrees, Declarations*. Edited by Austin Flannery. Northport, N.Y.: Costello Publishing, 1996.

———. *Lumen gentium*. Dogmatic Constitution on the Church. November 21, 1964.

———. *Unitatis redintegratio*. Decree. November 21, 1964.

———. *Perfectae caritatis*. Decree. October 28, 1965.

———. *Dignitatis humanae*. Declaration on Religious Liberty. December 7, 1965.

Vicaire, M-H. *L'Imitation des Apôtres: Moines, Chanoines et Mendiants*. Paris: Les Éditions du Cerf, 1963.

———. *The Apostolic Life*. Chicago, Ill.: Priory Press, 1966.

Vincent of Beauvais. *Speculum maius*. Vol. IV. Augsburg, 1474.

Waaijman, Kees. "Discernment and Biblical Spirituality: An Overview and Evaluation of Recent Research." *Acta Theologica* 33, Supplement 17 (November 2013): 1–12.

———. *The Mystical Space of Carmel: A Commentary on the Rule.* Translated by John Vriend. Louvain: Peeters, 1999.

Wawrykow, Joseph. "Creation." In *The Westminster Handbook to Thomas Aquinas.* Louisville, Ky.: Westminster Knox Press, 2005.

Welch, John, ed., *Carmel and Mary: Theology and History of a Devotion.* Washington, D.C.: Carmelite Institute, 2002.

Whybray, R. N. "Prophets/Ancient Israel." *The Oxford Companion to the Bible.* New York: Oxford University Press, 1993.

About the Authors

Keith J. Egan, T.O.Carm., is a Guest Professor in Theology at the University of Notre Dame and the Emeritus Aquinas Chair in Catholic Theology at Saint Mary's College (Ind.). He received his doctorate from Cambridge University where he studied under Dom David Knowles, OSB. He is the Past President of the Carmelite Institute and of the College Theology Society, Founder of the Center for Spirituality at Saint Mary's College, and a Corresponding Fellow of the Institutum Carmelitanum, Rome. He has published widely and lectured extensively in North America and Europe.

Steven Payne, OCD, is the endowed Chair of Carmelite Studies and ordinary professor of theology at The Catholic University of America. He received a doctorate in philosophy from Cornell University in 1982 and a doctorate in theology from The Catholic University of America in 2000. He is a priest of the Washington Province of the Discalced Carmelites. He is current president of the Carmelite Institute of North America, former principal of Tangaza University College (Kenya), former editor of *Spiritual Life* magazine and ICS Publications, and the author of *The Carmelite Tradition* (Liturgical Press, 2011) as well as numerous other works on Carmelite topics.

Index

Lightning Source UK Ltd.
Milton Keynes UK
UKHW010837221222
414021UK00005B/163